WE AIN'T TOO BRIGHT, ARE WE?

WE AIN'T TOO BRIGHT, ARE WE?

David G. Aragon

Print information available on the last page.

Rev. date: 01/30/2016

To order additional copies of this book, contact:
Xlibris
1-888-795-4274
www.Xlibris.com
Orders@Xlibris.com
564269

CONTENTS

"THE GOVERNMENT SHOULD FEAR

THE PEOPLE FOR THEY ARE ELECTED.

WHEN THE PEOPLE FEAR

THE GOVERNMENT YOU ARE

NO LONGER FREE"

THOMAS JEFFERSON 1801

WHERE ARE WE NOW?

DO THEY

FEAR US OR DO WE FEAR THEM?

READ AND VOTE

This book was written by a Christen, Constitutional conservative, middle class, construction worker, welder, mechanic, ranch hand, cowboy, educator, former president of a union local, shop steward and US Marine who cares about Americans and America. I wanted to let my feelings out as to what I see happening to this country. For this to be happening in this country, we couldn't be too bright. When people forget to use common sense, stop representing the people who voted them in, all in the name of lobbyists, special interest, lies, to be bought out to pass bills that spend money they don't have. When this country is set up to bring hard times on hard working Americans for power and money, America is in trouble.

When the news media sells out for high salaries to lie to Americans and not in their best interest, it's time you question what they are doing. When Americans are willing to give their lives for this country and come back from overseas duty and are said to be enemies of the state, along with people who still believe in religion, the Constitution, Bill of Rights, it's time to start questioning our leadership. When our leaders tell illegal aliens to break our laws, the laws they took an oath to defend, it's time we start looking for leaders who will uphold the laws.

Money doesn't make you rich but knowing right from wrong does, as does being willing to stand up for that your country that makes you richer. Our forefathers gave us that gift by doing just that; they stood up for this country with their blood. Freedom and the right to pursue happiness make you rich because if you use it right you'll find happiness. Money doesn't always give you that. Now the government thinks they know what's best for you. But as Jefferson said, "When the government acts under the pretense of taking care of you, you lose freedom and your rights". Now they are using backdoor tactics to take these rights away from you under the pretense they know what is better for you then you do and they'll protect us from ourselves. Why? Because we just ain't to bright are we?

I am richer than 95% of these rich people because I was blessed with a beautiful wife of 44 years, two sons, and two great daughter-in-laws, two grandsons and a miracle granddaughter, along with great families on both sides. I have friends from Mexico to Canada because I traveled competing in the sport I love and still compete in. I don't have to destroy people's lives for money and power. My family has had its hard times as well as its good times but we were willing to work them out for the betterment of the whole. All because of what our forefather taught us about freedom and our strong belief in God.

We now have people in government calling us a *dirty nation* (but look what this country has given them!) and yet they belittle it to other countries for their interest with no pride in what this country has done to make the world a better place. They point fingers while they are doing the same thing under the cover of their pointed fingers and Americans can't see for the words and promises and lies. All this because of certain smooth talking salespeople who has says just what people want to hear. Wake up before they spend you and your grand kids into a debt they never recover from! Wake up before the end of this country, as we know it and want to pass on to our future, is gone because of people wanting an elite ruling class. They are willing to divide this country with an old war tactic of divide and conquer, by using hate and prejudice to get the job done with not caring about the aftermath of what they have done. That's not what I call leadership, but greed. All we have to do to change for the better is get smart, find Americans who believe in Americans and America and vote them in. Not Politicians, but Americans with common sense and desire to make this once great country *great again*.

Vote in 2016 for a true change by voting us out of debt
by voting our congress out.

The Wisdom of Thomas Jefferson

---

1. When we get piled upon one on other in large cities, as in Europe, we shall become corrupt as Europe.
2. The democracy will cease to exist when you take away from those who are willing to work and give to those who would not.
3. It is incumbent on every generation to pay its own debts as it goes. A principle which if acted on would save one-half the wars of the world.
4. I predict future happiness for Americans if they prevent the government from wasting the labors of the people under the pretense of taking care of them.
5. My reading of history convinces me that most bad governments result from too much government.
6. No free man shall ever be debarred the use of arms.
7. The strongest reason for people to retain the right to keep and bear arms is, as a last resort, to protect themselves against tyranny in government.
8. The tree of liberty must be refreshed from time to time with the blood of patriots and tyrants.
9. To compel a man to subsidize with his taxes the propagation of ideas which he disbelieves and abhors is sinful tyranny.
10. I believe that banking institutions are more dangerous to our liberties than standing armies. If the American people ever allow private banks to control the issue of their currency, first by inflation, and then by deflation, the corporation that will grow up around banks

will deprive the people of property until their children wake-up homeless on the continent their forefather and father conquered.

Does this answer just how brilliant our forefathers were and how they saw what could happen? We are now letting our government do what he warned us about? How could we let this happen with all this out there to read? Don't teach Americans how to read!

Answer these questions but as you can see they warned us, *but we're not too bright, are we?*

We ain't too Bright, are we?

This is a book for people who think they are smart, but yet they cut off their nose to spite their face. I am not the brightest light on the tree but common sense and being able to read gives me the edge over most people. By the time you read this book you'll find out just how uninformed we are about the people running the government and just how not so bright we are. We have economic problems in this country, we have a government out of control, we have businesses failing, people losing jobs because the government is killing industry in this country, we have people lying to us about the weather and so on. But when it all comes down to it, we just ain't too bright.

If people would take the time to really find out the truth about things by just using common sense and looking things up, they'd find out lot more about the truth then listening to a snake-oil salesman or people whose only interest is they themselves. We all know our congressmen lie to us. Fact, one even told me that at my graduation. Picture this, a college graduation in a Baptist Church, a congresswoman at the pulpit, saying "The average American is not able to understand what happens in government therefore we have the right to lie to them".

Two questions come up from this statement. First, where in the Bible does it say if you get elected to the congress you can now break one of God's laws? Oh, I forgot, they are trying to take God out of everything now in congress. I must not be too bright. To think they should be held accountable for their action? But nowhere in the Bible does it say this. And the second question is "Do they think we are dumb?" The answer is, "Yes, they do."

And we are proving it by letting them do what they are doing; putting our grand kids and great- grand kids in debt for us with no end in sight.

Congress, Senate or House all feel the same way. Americans ain't too bright and we can pull the wool over their eyes any time we want. They just did it for trillions of dollars and we brought into it. They caused the problems by not acting on the problems before they became problems. Remember this was a congress that had a 9% rating because of lack of actions and we sent them back. We ain't too bright are we, and they know it.

First of all, Americans have got to remember what our forefathers set this country up as, *Republic* and second, *we, the American people are the government, not the elected people*. They are supposed to represent us as the *American People* and not the lobbyist, special interest or any foreign country or government but yet we let them be bought and sold by all the above. We ain't too bright. The only two things they represent are money and power. The Golden Calves of our politicians. We all know it and yet we vote them back in at 9% rating. We ain't too bright are we?

Why do we have 75,000 lobbyists in Washington D.C. who buy and sell our government to the highest bidder? We only have a little over 600 politicians and that many lobbyist, something wrong with the ratio here. The other thing is why do we need them, aren't these elected people smart enough to figure things that are good for Americans? (In fact they are not, just look at the result of their actions over the years) Have you noticed that most of them are lawyers? Isn't that letting the fox into the hen house? We ain't too bright are we for letting this happen. People who can't remember words just words and promises just promises, didn't our newly elected president promise to not have lobbyists in his cabinet. But better yet, he put a person who lobbied for arms in a pentagon to oversee that everything is done right. Fox in the hen house, or is he just paying off his debt to these lobbyists who gave him money for the election. By using common sense and a history of politics over the past few years we all know he is paying off his debt and not in the best interest of this country but in his best interest and also his other party interest.

The sky is not falling, the ocean not rising, nature is not falling apart(unless we look at all the government mistakes in handling nature because of special interest and money) but yet we believe what they are saying or printing. These people have only one interest and that is putting their ideals in place by buying our congress people. And they are for sale. All you have to do is promise them money for their election funds and you bought them. Or easier yet, just offer them $50,000 to speak in front of your meeting, an easy sale. But we are not too bright are we? We can't see this? No, we can't, because we elect them and send them back to congress. So we ain't too bright.

Over the last three elections voters have become cult members to their parties and can't see it. Yes, cult members. They forsake their church, forget about right and wrong, they put their party ahead of everything and they believe everything without question. Jim Jones would be proud of the parties for their cult members and the way they follow. The only difference is that they are losing their retirement, pension, and jobs because of the leadership in their cults today. But the thing they can't see is they are losing their rights and freedom because they just ain't too bright. This is a Republic, small central, strong state government.

People may say I am a Republican, *no, no, no*, I didn't vote for the last president at any point. I am smarter than that, I voted for someone I feel is better for the job. I voted for myself, and not Mr. Bush. Mr. Bush was just a Democrat in Republican clothing and you can see it in the bills he signed. The Democrats hate him because he did what they wanted to do and he was doing just that. He never vetoed bills with bad spending or pork. He signed bills that put people out of work and cost America a fifty-billion dollars industry and destroyed it just like Mr. Obama is doing now. President Obama is always saying we should look at France. Well, let's look at them; they use 75% nuclear power which we can't in America. They eat horse meat which we stopped shipping over because someone paid off our congress to kill a fifty-billion industry and put 500,000 workers out of work directly or indirectly. This entire bill was, special interest bill paid for people who have no clue about the truth and don't understand how it hurt the animals that they wanted to help. The government is also paying a half billion to feed these animals now. The only thing that got this bill passed is money, no facts, no worry about the outcome, and most of all no worry about the people it put out of work. Just because someone promised congressmen money for their re-election campaign and that's a good enough reason to sell Americans out.

Question: Where does it say in the Constitution that we tell the world what to eat and hurt Americans and cost them their jobs? Answer: Nowhere.

If you don't believe what I'm saying just ask yourself this. Why has Senator Dodd only receive $5000.00 from inside his state and $600,000.00 from people outside his state? If the people in his state were bright they'd be asking him who he represents; the citizen, of the state or the people who are buying him to do their bidding. But as you can see they ain't too bright they keep voting him back in. This is happening in all states and to all people running for office. Therefore they have a golden parachute waiting for them when they get out of congress because of doing their bidding. Haven't you noticed? We ain't too bright.

They talk about CEOs and their golden parachutes and Wall Street business hurting the country with greed and what are our politicians doing with their greed for power and money? Same damn thing. But yet we do nothing to them. Are they just better liars or are they better finger pointers? We had better figure it out before we lose everything. Yes, everything our forefathers gave us, freedom, bill of rights and the thing they swear to protect when they take the oath, The Constitution of the United States, and yet they are selling the Constitution down the river just for the belief of the few who have power and money backing them. We ain't too bright are we? With the support of the sale of America down the river, main stream news media are getting the job done. Americans will not see the light until someone shows them just how not to brightly they've been acting. Americans have become blinded by everything they have and the more they want just like the politicians have been blinded by their greed for power and money. Americans haven't seen how the government has become the power in this country and not the government of the people as it started out. Americans haven't asked why they are after the thing that our forefathers wrote about in all the papers written back then. Yes, God is their enemy because He makes them accountable and they don't want that. Accountable means no lies, working for the country and not special interest, no false gods like money and power, yes Americans have forgotten this and this book will hopefully remind them of that. If you read the old papers written by our forefathers, God was in every one of them but now we are trying to take Him out. If you want to see the true President Obama ask why at Georgetown Univ. he had them cover up the picture of Christ? Things American Christians don't know or hear about because the main stream media needs to keep his image intact. But religion took second place in this election as did the truth. Words just words and promises just promises that have already been broken by the President. They were easy to believe and not the truths because we ain't too bright are we? If the American people only knew what laws our congressmen break and were told by the main stream media, they'd come after them with the pitchfork and not the bankers. But if God was back in the government, like in the beginning, I wouldn't be writing this book would I?

The sad story in this whole thing is that if they'd look at history it'll tell us the story and we would *change* for the betterment of this country. But we are only listening and never hearing the truth. Why can't we hear the truth? Well, our politicians know why we just ain't too bright. The last time people protested on tax day or people talked against the government, it was *freedom of speech*. It wasn't called into question by the people but main stream media did. If you call the actions of the government into question now-a-days you are a militant. Sounds familiar? Or in other people's eyes you are now prejudice. Funny how they can call people who oppose them those names, but when they did it, they were only using their first amendment rights and now we're militants. See how quickly things and standards change. But again, you voted for *change,* didn't you?

If we just couldn't hear the truth and become bright again.

Basically this book is about the following things:

1. Calling into question why is our government trying to take over everything in this country and trying to control of Americans and their livelihoods?
2. Why are they trying to destroy our Constitution and Bill of Rights, and take or destroy our belief in God, making us a second rate country or in their words just part of a global government?
3. Why are they selling out to the idea of becoming part of a world government?
4. Why are they saying the sky is falling?
5. We'll take a look at hate and prejudice in this country and see how to end it.
6. We'll take a look at a better way to solve our economic problem without going into debt for the future.
7. How to solve the true educational problem in this country without the lies?

A lot of these issues overlap so you may see it covered twice and maybe even three or more times but the issues can be solved with common sense and hard work. But the biggest question I have for them is why if we are considered the *greatest nation* in the world, are we selling out to become a second or third rate world country? How could we have voted for this to happen? If the truth was know we didn't. It was *words just words and promises just promises,* and the hope for *change* for the betterment of the country. We only listened and didn't hear a word of truth from them but what they promised ain't happening for the better. Lost jobs, lost homes, lost industries and now even lost hope. How can we change it for the betterment of Americans? Read, hear and take action.

GOVERNMENT

Let's take a hard look at the government we now have in place. Spend, lie and what else to benefit themselves and the people who bought them? If you remember, in the first chapter I talked about an elected official who said it was ok the lie to the *Americans* because they didn't understand the truth about government; in other words we ain't too bright. For years now we've all known they lie to us yet we send them back to Washington D.C. Why? We're just not getting it, or are we really not that bright?

There was a cute movie; I believe it was around 1939 release. The Lady and the Cowboy. Gary Cooper was the star but I can't remember the lady. The story was about a rich girl who wanted to go to a rodeo. So she took her maids, met a cowboy, fell in love, married and next the problem. Her dad was thinking of running for president. In the meantime she had moved to Montana with her uninformed husband about who she was. For some reason she went back to Calif. to get the rest of clothes but ended up staying longer she needed. So he being the loving husband, goes after her. Goes to the house where he believed her to have worked at, knocks on the door and is told to go to the back door. Being the gentleman and cowboy, he goes to the back door where the maids who had gone out with her, were working. They said she had gone, but he heard her voice in the other room and forced his way in. There at the table she was talking to her father and finally introduced him as her husband. Now being rich and having not a clue as to what was happening in real life, they started belittling the trade of being a cowboy. At which point he told them, "If you get off your high horse and stop looking down your noses at people because they don't

—
19

live the way you do and really find out what works for them, maybe then they could understand people and do a better job as government (elected) officials." So you can see this problem has been around for years and elected officials still forget where they came from and who they represent.

Take Senator Dodd running for re-election in his home state. He has only received 5000.00 from voters in his home state and 600,000.00 from outside his state. Here is some of the questions I'd be asking myself if I lived in that state.

1. Why do people from outside his state want him to win, and why would put that kind of money up?

2. What are they getting out of him for their money?

3. If they are willing to spend that kind of money, does he really represent them or is just bought and paid for to get his vote on issues they have nothing to do with what's right or wrong with this country, only someone buying another vote?

4. Is this what's wrong with our election system that anyone with money can buy what they need from our elected officials?

5. Are all elected officials bought and paid for? This one is all Americans, Demo. or Rep. to answer.

I saw one of Bill Clinton's top advisors in an interview say just that. In his own words that most of them are bought and paid for before they get to Washington. And now you know the rest of the story. So they represent the money as if we didn't know, but we're not too bright because we sent them back.

Let's take a look at just what happen over the last six months. First you got to understand that a lot of these things have happening over years to make it possible, because they just don't happen. Oct. surprise was not a surprise because when Hilary lost the primary, she warned us of the Oct. surprise. If they knew about it, why didn't congress try and head it off or just tell us this was to come? Where was the main stream media? Both candidates being in the senate, they should have known and why didn't they debate this issue before it happened? John McCain's warning of the over site committees not doing their jobs in 2005 and Bill Clinton saw the problem coming in 1998-99 and asked for help from both parties and nothing came of their cries for action. So, as you can see, they in no way represent Americans, but special interests who have brought and paid for them. But we ain't too bright, are we?

Here's some other interesting tit bits, like who said money is best made in a recession? Or who backed certain candidates and helped; who later came out with statements that started a rush on a bank in Calif.? Warren Buffet backed President Obama, and he said money can be made in a recession if you have money and who has money? Soros backs a lot of candidates. One came out and made a statement that a bank in Calif. was going to fail and there was a rush to it; the bank failed and Soros now owns it. Do your own math. But all of these statements came from former Washington insiders, if you really want to do the research. So the idea that this administration has nothing to do with Wall Street is shown as not true.

The thing is here that it doesn't matter as to what state you represent the key to staying in Washington, D.C. and who's pockets you can grease and they'll grease yours right back. But this isn't something Americans haven't heard before or didn't know about, is it? But we ain't too bright because knowing all this we still send them back to represent us even if we know they don't.

Here's a question nobody's asked. Why were both parties so afraid of Governor. Palin? Well, here's something to think about. What would have been her job in Washington DC? She would have been in the senate to oversee it. The committees, the bills and everything else, she would have had something to do with it. She was an outsider, never played the game, and cleaned a lot of things up in Alaska. What do you think they were afraid of? She would have pointed out the things that they were doing or not doing, that has nothing to do with making things better in America.

John McCain was giving you a gift of someone who could have given you real change in Washington. But you let the main stream media and politicians, who no longer represent Americans, destroy true change for words just words and promises just promises; but as usual we weren't too bright. We couldn't see a gift horse or lipstick moose if we looked it in the eye. But again we are not too bright, are we?

—

Just think of someone that probably would have fought for Americans and not special interests. Right from wrong but not being too bright we are now being sold out as a country by someone who must hates this country the way it is so he's going to give it a complete makeover. The word "sorry" sure comes out of his mouth a lot. Don't get me wrong, we have made a lot of mistakes because of our leadership or lack of leadership is that has caused it.

As Americans we have always been willing to help out any country and that has been proven in war after war and in need of aid, time and time again. We never asked to be repaid for the lives we have lost. And like that old saying, "the good has always outweighed the bad in the end".

So, yes, they attacked her because in the real world meaning of change, she would have been that. So how low has the politicians and the main stream media gone? Well, when you start lying about people and tilt the stories to hurt someone because if the truth were known, they'd be caught in another lie. Who did we trust at one time but no longer? Mainstream media! Sad, under the Constitution freedom of speech was set up to help protect us and now, well, it's to control us, lie to us, see if they can trick people to get the answers they want. We all known the main stream media thinks we ain't too bright. Better yet they know we ain't too bright.

How many voters can remember the Democrats putting off the voting on off shore drilling and drilling for oil in this country before the election. They went home, most of them promised off shore drilling and domestic drilling to get elected.

Anyone heard of off shore drilling and the Democrats; they just pushed a bill that cut off 2 million acres of prime oil reserves. So much for campaign promises. And you really want to get angry, throw in the buy outs because they ain't working for us. But again we ain't too bright.

Going back to the Oct. surprise, which was not a surprise, again we could have gotten out of this with no money being spent, by using common sense but congress had to pay its debts back. Again questions you have got to ask yourself about all that's happened. Why was it rushed through? Why so much pork? Why all the lies about the companies that we were buying out? Why didn't they take the time to check everything out before they acted? Didn't all this rushing thing cause you any alarm or are you just not too bright? Because I know you don't trust congress because it only had a 9% rating.

The second buy out was just more pork. How does paying Acorn 5 billion dollars to create jobs? Or was it just a payout for the election? Why did the three Republicans change side after they got more pork for their states? Didn't they change their minds just to stay in Washington or because of no backbone? Cause all they did was put the taxpayers back in the home state deeper in debt. Jobs are still being lost, people are still losing their homes, and our grand kids are now in debt because of us not saying stop. How could congress pass a bill without reading it? So do you think they acted in your best interest? I doubt it. But again we ain't too bright.

Where are we cutting the federal budget? What departments are making the biggest cuts? Do you think going around the world and telling the rest of the world just how bad we are, helps us? Do you think going after people who had to do something after 9-11 will change anything or maybe they are just letting Americans know that they hate Americans enough to put people in jail just things they say, mess with us and this can and will happen to you? Do you think saying people coming back from overseas after a tour of duty are militia, is true? Or are they just starting a new group to hate that they think can come back and vote against them? The ones they are afraid of are the ones that are willing to give their lives to protect your freedom and the Constitution of this once great country. Do you think that acting from weakness and is good for this country? If you believe this, I got some ocean front property in New Mexico I'll sell you. Or are we not too bright? Why is the government so high on the sky is falling? When our leader is saying we are not a Christian country when we were founded on that belief. He claims to be a Christian and then makes that statement. What's wrong with this picture?

Ask yourself why in less than a 100 days under this president, we have all these questions to ask ourselves. It doesn't make a difference if you a Demo. or Rep., if you are rich or poor, from the country or city, no one in Washington is acting in you best interest. And the biggest question and probably the most important one is: Why are the Demo. always push hate and prejudice to win and elect? This is an old war tactic to divide and conquer but it is tearing this country in two. So I am going to give you an answer to end hate and prejudice if they really want to (which I doubt). I'll do this with science and history.

First off all there is only one race . . . It doesn't matter if you are a Christian or believe in creation. I am an organ donor. If President Obama becomes sick because of a kidney problem and needed his kidney changed out. He and I matched and I was killed in an accident (God forbid). Guess what would happen? They'd pull my kidneys, fly them to where he is and put them in him. Doesn't matter about the color or where I came from, we match. Humans are interchangeable because there is only one race. Second, in science the body can change to meet the climate. Thus in warm areas dark skin and in cold areas light skin. Do you remember what hate and prejudice is, nothing more than fear and not being too bright.

Do you ever watch kids? They don't care what you look like all they do is want to play. Or old People, they also don't care, all they want is a friend but the Democrats want everyone to hate just to divide and stay in power.

The next lesson is a history lesson. Blacks in Africa sold blacks into slavery.

They didn't care who all bought them; all they wanted to do is get rid of their enemies. It was what they did back then. In the 1860's we had a war is this country dividing the country in half. One believed that all men were created equal and the other didn't. Families were torn apart. Right and wrong, it did matter?

Question: How many blacks fought for the North? Maybe about five percent, the rest were white people who gave two things in This War. First, they gave Blacks freedom and the right to become Americans. Second, some of them gave the greatest gift that they could give, their lives to say that all men are equal.

Question: What do the Black owe the families of the men that died for men to be equal? They didn't set them free to become slave to government handouts or People telling them someone owes them something. No, they set them free to live and dream and build a better life for themselves but hate dies hard, when you have politicians and politics trying to enslave you again just for your vote. Yes, that what we have here in America. Why do you think that we have never fought a big drug war? Why do you think education has failed in this area? On this you'll find out more when I cover education.

As you can now see, our government isn't the one that tries and stops hate but pushes it for one reason and one reason only, to win election. You want to end hate and prejudice, vote out this government, for a government that doesn't have the false Gods of power and greed. Here's how you do it and it's so easy. The number one reason we must REMEMBER IS THERE IS ONLY ONE RACE, THE HUMAN RACE, WE ARE ALL CREATED IN GOD IMAGE, the second one is, all forms change to the following two questions. First

1. If born in another country than America fill out._____.

2. What date did you become a citizen? _____

Then you know where they came from and who they are. But you don't divide them into race or anything else; just a human being and being Americans which they are.

Remember your surname only tells you where you came from not who or what you are. If you were born in this country, then you are an *American,* that's it.

Doesn't matter where your parents came from, you are an American. Color has nothing to do with it but if you want hate and prejudice to continue just listen to your government and politicians, it will sure help keep it alive. They need you to stay divided or you may figure out they're not there for your best interests. And right now they hate the Greatest Papers ever written next to the Bible. Your Constitution and Bill of Rights!

If you ever take God out of our life, like they are doing in Washington right now, then no one is accountable and they will push hate and prejudice even more.

As you can see, now they have new targets for people to go after. People believe in the Constitution, guns, religion, military or any who doesn't see this country as they do.

Maybe you haven't noticed how government is getting into all areas of your life from what and how we eat to what we can do. A few have been good but the rest are just used to control us. Fear has been used so many time to pass laws; they only take freedom anyway. 9 out of 10 times the government has created the problems.

Maybe we should take a hard look at "the sky is falling" or as they call it "global warming." Ask yourself this: If plants need CO2 to make O2 and we need plants for food for animals and ourselves, why is it bad? If plants are converting CO2 it into O2, the thing that helps give us life, again how is it bad? If the government is now trying to make pollution to cool the earth down, isn't that a good reason to keep auto makers and industries going strong? Why are they saying one thing in one department and then saying just the opposite in another one, sometimes in the same breath or I guess they know we ain't too bright and think we'd believe everything they say. If you look at the environmentalist and animal rights people who for some reason have money to buy our congressmen and get bills passed with no real research or findings out the true outcome. I could show you so many common sense ways to protect the environment from the mistakes that these groups of people are paying for and not doing the job. They just sound good.

But here's the other question: If less people feel the same way about things and common sense has a better answer, why are they getting passed? The political answer is for the best interest of the country but the true answer is I now have money to run for office again. We all know it. They know we know it, but they also know we ain't too bright and that we ain't going to do nothing about it.

They know as long as they can buy a six pack of beer, watch TV, football or other sports and maybe watch mainstream media news, Americans ain't bright enough to know what's happening to them and one day they'll wake and find themselves living in a country with little or no rights left. And it will be done in the names of environment, safety, health, but it will be the same thing, government control.

If you watch the news lately, overweight people are causing global warming and they are giving dozens of reasons why. When are the lies and fear tactics are going too ends? The problem they have now is that only thirty percent of Americans believe in global warming and it's becoming a something they are afraid may come apart on them.

Remember Al Gore and his mini-minds were challenged and the only thing he could say was the research has to be done by Americans scientists. These were scientists from around the world who made the challenge. If you know a lot about the grants that our scientists get, it's about proving the government right or no money. But we ain't too bright, are we?

Banks can't pay money back to the government now to get out from under them. Why? You'd think they'd want it back. Not if it meant losing control of those banks. People don't put 1 and 1 together because if they did they'd see the truth. I always knew my math was going to get me in trouble. But most of us ain't too bright.

It's time to move on to the next chapter because if you read this you're beginning to do the math and it ain't too pretty, is it? But here is the kicker that you haven't heard about yet and you tell me if you think what I'm saying now is bad, just wait.

Did you know we are only one of a few countries that hasn't signed a world treaty on how to raise our children? To make sure you understand this UN will now tell us how to raise our kids. Guess what your government's thinking of signing? Guess what this will mean to you and the way you raise your kids? If signed, government can now tell you just how to do it as set by the world. We've been raising our kids for thousands of years, do you think they need to tell us how?

And why is mainstream media not saying anything about this *Treaty* or covering something this important to Americans? But as you know by now, we just ain't too bright.

Did you know that there are court cases that the judges have ruled against the parents in this country, forcing parents to change their habits to meet the wants of the child over what they feel is right. Where in our Constitution does it say that the government knows more about raising our kids than we do? What standards are they going to go by? Hopefully not their standards, because they failed at everything. But remember the old saying, "if you want something to fail just give it to the government." What did we do in the last election because of words, just words and promises just promises? Again proving we are not too bright.

Another senator just proved what I am writing about is true. Senator Specter just changed from the Republican party to Democratic. Here's what I'd be asking if I live in that state. What did they promise him? He knew he was going to lose if he stayed Rep. Is this the kind of person I want in Washington? What's coming down the road that makes him think that by changing parties he can win now? Because of his change there are no more checks and balance in the senate. How's that for selling out Americans? As long as he stayed in the Rep. Party there was the hope of stopping bad bills from being passed but no longer. The damage he has just done to the people he said he represented is so great this country may never be able to recover from this move. He must have gotten some kind of promise because not only did he sell out the people he represented but the nation and the Constitutions.

Most of all, he sold out the future generations of this country in hopes he could stay in Washington with power and greed. But if the truth was known he is 78 and wants to stay in Washington no matter who buys him off. It doesn't have to be money all the time and that's what worries me.

Going a little bit more into the bills Washington is looking at is cap and trade, which is really a tax bill on CO_2. All this is going to do is have our electric bills go up with no end in the near future. It'll only makes times harder on Americans that are now having a rough time paying their bills. Question: Is this the Democratic way of making Americans so they are more likeable because they are being put in their place by a government who has no idea what made this country great? Did we vote for more taxes? Is that what we said when this election was over? I believe that most of them ran promising less tax. Or was it a play on words? No more income taxes for a short time. Then we are going to hit you hard after we are elected. Question: Now with no one to stop them from passing anything they want, do you think they care what you think? But again we ain't too bright. Words just words, promises just promises and lies just lies.

Every day things happen that are setting up to take away more of our liberties and freedoms given to us by our forefathers. Is this what we voted for when Americans voted for change? Or were we just sold a bill of goods because they think we are not too bright. I think they believe we're not too bright and there is very little room to hang on now because of what just happened. WE BETTER BRIGHTEN UP.

Fore-Warned

THE BRILLIANCE OF OUR FOUNDING FATHERS

Can we understand just how brilliant our founding fathers were? They warned us about everything that would happen if we stopped teaching our children about the Constitution and the Bill of Rights. They also warned us that if we didn't pay attention to what happens in our government, we'd lose our freedom. So I plan to inform you about what they warned us in their writings. So let's start with the main guy.

George Washington

"THE POWER UNDER THE CONSTITUTIONWILL ALWAYS BE WITH PEOPLE. It is entrusted for defined purposes, and limited periods, to representatives of their own choosing; and whenever it is executed contrary to their interest, not agreeable to their wishes, their servants can, and undoubtedly will be, recalled."

Take a look at that statement. What is it saying to the people? If they don't do the job we hired them for, you'll fire them. We the people don't fire them, we send them back, we get the same result, send them back, get the same results and we send them back again. Now they are being paid for by different people, businesses, countries, lobbyists, special interest, and anybody who wants to buy them. We the people end up getting the lies, promises, and short end of the stick. By the end of this book you'll see how you can change that. But another question you better ask yourself, are you willing to help make the change, because if you aren't, this country is even in bigger trouble then you think.

In the 2014 election we told them what we wanted, we gave them what they needed and they kicked us in the teeth. Plain and simple; stop the health care, stop the immigration, stop the spending, no more taxes, what did we get but more spending, more immigration, and now they want more taxes.

Some of this is from a man who said before his first election that it a crime to spend more money than you take in, this will put your country in deep debt. What has he done to this country? Doubted the debt on his own, passed laws that he couldn't and congress has just let him and for kickers, they funded all of the above when we asked them not too. So why would we even think about sending anyone of them back in the next election? Are we insane?

"On every question of construction, (let us) carry ourselves back to the time when the Constitution was adopted, recollect the spirit manifested in the debates, and instead of trying what meaning may be squeezed out of the text, or invented against it, conform to the probable one in which it was passed." Thomas Jefferson

What have the democrats and the republicans done in the last few years? They have turned this country upside down with their own ideas. What this statement says, read why it written the way it was, don't change the meaning, but the politicians have tried for their benefits to meet their needs. Basically what our elected officials are saying is "we the ruling class and Americans aren't as smart as us so we write the laws for us to stay in power."

What has the Supreme Court Justices done in the last few findings or ruling, on health care, marriage and religion? Wouldn't you say they twisted it around to meet the needs of the Party and not the people? I don't think they remember they work for us and not the parties, but us, do they? We the People are the government in the Constitution, not the courts, not politicians, but We the People. Why don't we start being the government by voting them out? We can do that, by finding Candidates, not politicians, but candidates, who can do the job of working for the people. Not Governors, or Senators, who are politicians working their way up a career for them, but why not Americans who want the job to get the job done and walk away. It's not a career, but we let them make it a career by voting them back in time and time again. We have term limits in Constitution, why don't we use them as they were set up by our founding fathers. JUST VOTE THEM OUT PERIOD. Or are we, just ain't too bright.

Most of the founding fathers believed in God put His hand on all of what was written with Divine intervention. Now our government is trying to take God out of it. Why? Why are they afraid of God?

"...I am committed against thing which, in my judgment, may weaken, endanger, or destroy(the constitution)... and especially against the all extension of Executive power; and I am committed against any attempt to rule the free people of this country by power and the patronage of the government itself..."

"It is hardly too strong to Say that the Constitution was made to guard the people against the dangers of good intentions. There are men in all ages who mean to govern well, but they mean to govern. They promise to be masters, but they mean to be masters." Both statements by: Daniel Webster

What is President Obama doing now? Is he not running the country by Executive action? Because our Republicans leaders are too weak and have no clue of what our founding fathers and the Constitution was sat it up to protect the people of this country. These are just a few of the many things that are going on in Washington D.C. that is hurting the country and we the people.

The answers to these questions come from Thomas Jefferson.

"In questions of power, then, let no more be heard of confidence in the man, but bind him down from mischief by the chains of the Constitution."

Again, it is made clear, the rules are set in the Constitutions and when you break them you must go back to the way it is sat down in the Constitution. But to do that you must understand and believe in the Constitution. Just ask yourself this question. The Tea Party believes in the Constitution, they believe in small government as the country was founded but both party called the Tea Party people trouble makers for believing in the Constitution which limits government to what it can do. The politicians don't want limit, they want lies, promises, and working for the ruling class, not for we the people. When you use the word CAN'T it means you don't want to do it or won't do it.

Thomas Jefferson on debt:

"to preserve our independence, we must not let our rulers load us with perpetual debt... I am for a government rigorously frugal and simple."

Where are we now with our debt? With debt and borrowing, what are congress and this President trying to do to stop this from getting us in worth shape? Government is taking our debt even higher than ever before and no stopping in sight. Letting the caps on spend go up, borrowing more, taxing the working class, and best of all is say we in Washington are the government. Go back to George Washington and the Constitution. We the people are the government, not one word of a ruling class or even governing class.

HERE IS WHAT SOME OF OUR FOUNDING FATHERS SAID WOULD CAUSE TO LOSE OUR COUNTRY.

"Only a virtuous people are capable of freedom. As a nation become corrupt and vicious, they have need of masters." Benjamin Franklin

"All tyranny needs to gain a foothold is for people of good conscience to remain silent."

Thomas Jefferson

How would you like to hear how we could change this? This is what our founding fathers believed, we the people are the government, here is what we the people need to do to control what is happening in this country and get it back on track. It'll take hard work, but we the people are the government, not the President, who believe it's his way and that he's the smartest man in the room. Next to these guys, he ain't too bright.

"A well-instructed people alone can be permanently a free people." James Madison

Here are the most important ones.

"A primary object...should be the education of our youth in the science of government. In the Republic, what species of knowledge can be equally important? And what more pressing ...than communicating it to those who are to be the future guardians of the liberties of the country?" George Washington

"I know of no safe depositor of the ultimate powers of (a) society but the people themselves; and if we think them not enlightened enough to exercise their control with a wholesome discretion, the remedy is not to take it from them, but inform their discretion by education. This is the true corrective of abuses of the Constitutional powers." Thomas Jefferson

"Say ...whether peace is best preserved by giving energy to the government or information to the people. This last is the most certain and the most legitimate engine of government. Educate and inform the whole mass of people. Enable them to see that it is their interest to preserve peace and order, and they will preserve them. They are the only sure reliance for the preservation of our liberty." Thomas Jefferson

Now you know what the founding fathers were thinking when they wrote the Constitution. Now let's take a look at some of the things they wrote Constitution.

1. THE PRESIDENT MUST TAKE THE OATH BEFORE BECOMING PRESIDENT. "Before he enters on the Execution of his of his office he shall take the following Oath or Affirmation; I do solemnly swear that I will faithfully execute the Office of President of the United States and will to the best of my Ability, preserve, protect and defend the Constitution of the United States"

2. Congress shall control the money, not the President.

3. The one thing they did say, "We the people are the government, not the elected official, they are to representatives the people who vote them in."

If people would only read the Constitution and the writings of the founding fathers, they would see how our elected officials are failing to do their job for us. And if we would stop being Dems or Rep. and start becoming Americans again all this would end by voting them all

out. WE THE PEOPLE ARE THE GOVERNMENT, JUST ASK OUR
FOUNDING FATHERS.

Now I'm going to show what our founding fathers believed would
destroy this government, this country, and take your freedoms away
from the people if our leaders did the following actions. Than you
have to ask yourself again, is this happening in this country under our
elected officials?

"The democracy will cease to exist when you take away from those
who are willing to work and give to those who would not." Thomas
Jefferson

What are we talking about when we talk about spreading the wealth,
stealing from the people who are willing to work and giving to those
who aren't? When congress passes a bill cutting you work down to 29
hrs. no longer 40 hrs., and tells you, you're better off, someone trying
to pull the wool over your eyes or figure you just ain't too bright. You
work hard to get ahead and the government is now kicking you in the
teeth. Both sides!

"It is incumbent on every generation to pay its own debts as it
goes. A principle which if acted on would save one-half the wars of
the world." TJ

The President made the statement about President Bush taking us
into debt, it's on American, unpatriotic, he has now in his term doubt
the of every president before him and with his new budget, asking
congress to raise the debt limit, he is going to take us deeper in debt.
The Republicans will give him that new limit because they are not
working for the people that voted them in. The same president who
lost both house and was told to cut our debt along with congress who
was told to cut our debt, seem like the didn't hear a word the American
people told them.

"I predict the future happiness for Americans, if they prevent the
government from wasting the labors of the people under the pretense
of taking care of them." TJ

What is welfare, foods stamps, now the health care bill, isn't that
set up to take care of us? Why did we need change? We had the best
health care in the world. Here's the part that the older Americans
should really be angry about. Social Security, Medicare was paid into

by us to assure we had a medical program and retirement program set aside for people in their retirement years. One start in the 40's and the other in the 60's, each pay check the government took money out of our checks, in the 60's President Johnson started stealing from SS for his war on poverty and the stealing hasn't stop. (So much for a locked box) The reason they steal from it is because of one word. Tax (FICA tax) This puts the money in the general fund, and that allows them to steal from it. So much for the government watching out for us, right! Add that to President stealing from that fund now to take care of the illegal people who have never paid a penny into it. Oh yah, did they also tell it's run out of fund? So now, it'll run out sooner than later. As you're learning here our politicians think our money is their money to spend. Both parties!

"Reading of history convinces me that most government results from too much government." TJ

This explains itself.

Read Carefully

"I believe that banking institutions are more dangerous to our liberties then a standing armies. If the American people ever allow private banks to control the issue of their currency, first by inflation, and then by deflation, the corporation that will grow up around banks will deprive the people of property until their children wake-up homeless on the continent their forefathers and fathers conquered."

What has happen in 2008 when the housing collapse, didn't we learn anything from that. Why are we letting it happen again? If we don't get our financial system under control, spending and debt under control this country is going to fail and is taking us down that road? (the PRESIDENT and congress or better yet both parties) We ain't too bright, are we? We elect them back in, don't we?

"The strongest reason for people to retain the right to keep and bear arms is, as a last resort, to protect themselves against tyranny in government." TJ

Our forefathers knew that someday someone would come along wanting to destroy the Constitution, freedom it guarantees, and enslave the people to a ruler, dictator, or a group of people who believe they were smarter and should be the ruling class of people. If you look around you'll find that we are at that point now. If you remember from this chapter, you were warned about this in their writings. This was the way they fought back in those days. To fight back today we the people must educate Americans and start putting our money where our mouth is, find good American candidates and vote both parties out. We don't need to elected Demos and Rep. but Americans who believe in our Constitution, our freedoms and that this is the GREATNESS COUNTRY IN THE WORLD. But you have to ask why the Democrats and the President are fighting so hard to take our rights, guaranteed by the Constitution, to own and bear arms. Answer that question and you know why this country is in trouble.

Start by finding out the truth. OUR ELECTED OFFICIALS ARE BOUGHT AND PAID FOR BY LOBBYIST, THE RICH, SPECIAL INTEREST GROUPS, FOREIGN GOVERNMENT AND ANY ONE ELSE WHO HAS THE MONEY TO BUY THEM. On one of the news station a person was talking on bills are passed. Basically he said that the people what paid for the bill wrote the bills and congress passes the bills. A representative government is the elected to represent the people who voted them in, not the money, not the party, not special interest, or any other people who wants to control the government by buying the elected officials. Most people in Washington D.C. believe they are the ruling class and have forgotten what the CONSTITUTION WAS WRITTEN FOR; WE THE PEOPLE ARE THE GOVERNMENT. The people have to want to become Americans first and not party members.

Economy and Control

Why didn't either party see the fall coming or did they and did nothing thinking this was normal? The answer seems that they did nothing just as before. But if you look at congressional records and statements by past presidents, congress refused to act on this issue. Again a do- nothing congress has shown us just how not so bright we are in this country. We voted them back in because we only listen to the words and promises but did not hear the truth even as they told it. We couldn't see the lies even if we knew they were lying because we are now cult members. So now we are losing jobs, income, going to be paying more taxes, and lose our freedom all in the name of the environment, health, economy, and the need for government to takeover to stop failure. Question: Doesn't the government always fail and if so, how can they say they can save us? Because they believe we ain't too bright.

Why aren't we fighting mad at the politicians in Washington who passed a major spending bill without reading? What is the first thing a lawyer tells you to do before signing any contract? Read it. Why didn't they read it? What were they trying to hide? Was this bought out also used to pay back debts to people who supported the politicians? Was the 5 billion dollars planned to go Acorn for the things they did in the election even if several charges were against them for illegal actions during the election? Why are congressmen not willing to investigate these cases? What are they trying to hide from us by preventing an investigation in this organization with ties to government money? Why are they buying out bad banks they forced to make bad loans just to get elected and now that's going to be paying the price? When are we going to cut off the government credit card that seems to never end? Did you know you could do that? Start calling them, start asking for their records on how they voted on issues and take it back to them if they are running for re-election and letting them know we know the truth.

If records aren't let out you now know they have something to hide. What it all comes down to is all they want is control and the money they get for voting for someone who paid them for their re-election. Therefore the control is number one in their minds. Why didn't we just let the banks, Freddie and Fanny and AIG just fail and file for bankruptcy? Well if you truly follow the money you'll see a lot it end up in the hands of politician's hands for re-election. What was really hidden in this bill? Franks, Dodd, Obama and many other congressmen got great amounts of money from these companies. Why didn't they go after the people who made large amount of money in Fanny and Freddie, those who walked away with millions? Two of President Obama's top advisors were former CEOs of Freddie and Fanny. Why did Fanny and Freddie top people get their bonus and not the AIG top people? Why wasn't there an outcry about this? Answer: The news media didn't cover it because they knew it would anger Americans and they couldn't have that. Lies again, control of media again, control of people. Why did we have different standards for bonuses in two companies that the government bailed out? Follow the money for re-elections and you'll get some of the answers. But are we just not too bright?

What if we started drilling for oil off- shore, and any other place we have oil. What if we started turning coal into gas and diesel? What if we started using nuclear power for electricity?

Well, we could become oil independent and stop the export of 700 billion dollars and maybe stop going deeper into debt. But knowing the government they'll come with an excuse like, we wouldn't want the world to go into a recession, or we got to protect the earth from us dirty

Americans. What if we admitted the sky wasn't falling, the earth not warming and why are we cutting off our noses? Why would President Obama top men in the environment say we have to create volcanoes to put pollution in the air to cool the environment down? Couldn't we just do that by letting Americans drive gas vehicles, let factories work, phase out electricity with coal generators? Aren't they saying one thing to get another with this statement? Aren't you thinking common sense tells you to do just that; let things stay the same and we wouldn't have to build volcanoes at a great cost to us? Isn't it true that only 30% of Americans believe the earth is warming and if that's the case, why aren't the rest fighting back the lies? Control and power rule.

If you can read, just read a seventh- grade science book. It'll tell you that oil has been leaking into the ocean for thousands of years. That carbon di-oxide is taken into plants to produce oxygen, the thing that gives us life. Why would President Obama top men on the environment say that if we wanted to cool down the earth, we'd need to put pollution into the air by building volcanoes and cause pollution to go into air? Why don't we just drive the gas vehicles, make the pollution and keep American auto-workers working, keep industry working and keep the cost of electricity low. But no we just like lying to the Americans who ain't too bright. You see common sense can solve a lot of these problems without spending hard- working Americans' money just to cause change. But what would do this do? Put Americans back to work, start the economy growing again and get back to normal. Let's even go one step more, President Obama said we should look at France and I agree.

So let's look at France. 75% of their electric power comes from nuclear power which we should be using here. It's clean, available in large supply and can help this country. They also eat horse meat which was a 50 billion dollars industry which was closed because someone brought the votes to close it. It also put 500,000 workers out of work directly and indirectly. We also now pay out a half billion dollars to feed the horses that people couldn't take care for, for one reason or another. They never looked at the harm, the truth or what would happen to them if they passed these bills. These bills were just passed because someone paid big money to your congressmen and just as they didn't read the big spending bill, they had no clue as to the facts of what would happen; just the lies told to them by people with money which they wanted some of and they didn't worry about the outcome. This money comes from speeches, re-election campaign funds or anywhere else that they can cover up legally. They passed the laws, remember. But again we ain't too bright are we? This is just an example of what your government has done to the kill the economy we have and it happened with a Democratic congress and a so called rancher- president. Your answer to the questions is, "they didn't look at facts".

What if we let the banks that made bad loans file for bankruptcy? Tell credit unions and small banks to re-finance the loans and government would back them. As the loans start getting approved, the banks in trouble would start getting some of their money back and can now start over, only this time without government telling them to make the bad loans. Common sense tells us there are other ways to do things but the government isn't about common sense. You can sure bet congress ain't that bright or are they? They just sold us out and we haven't tried to tell them not to continue on this track. If you can't see it by now not just one party has messed up. If you remember the Democrats needed two votes and three Rep. sold out on the buyout. They got more pork for themselves to stay in office. This was just proven again by Senator Specter who just left the Rep. Party and became a Demo because he knew he had no chance of getting re-elected if he stayed in the Rep. Party. They are willing to sell out our great- grand kids just to stay in office, doesn't speak very highly for of them representing the people does it? But we ain't too bright.

Take a short look at the AIG buy out. 250 billion dollars went over sea right off the bat. If they would have gone with bankruptcy, they wouldn't have had to pay that money back until they got back on their feet, saving us billions in the buyout. Common sense not panics. Our government couldn't let Wall Street's poorly run companies to go under because they get too much money from them for election and re-election. You don't cut off the hand that feeds you, do you? But we ain't too bright. What they did was sell out the average Americans to protect their money source for them to gain power and money. Another thing is, have you noticed how our government always backs failure. That's not what most Americans want is it? If you're starting to notice I'm giving you solutions that don't spend your hard-earned money by using common sense. Gee, maybe if we got people with common sense we could have real change as promised but we aren't getting. Now the car industry which was once our sign of strength is now being run down because of lies about the global warming and if you want to tear a country down go for its strength and they have. Think about this. Why are we not working at changing the environment by letting our scientists and engineers do what they have the knowledge to do? Over time all things will be taken care of. Instead of panicking about what will happen after thousands of years it's time we started looking at a little change expected in one hundred years. Haven't they reduced pollution, produced better vehicles and kept our country productive and that has been done in the last twenty years. So why are we letting the government panic us with lies that they will not debate with scientists from outside America. Because they have something to hide. All they really want is control and not an answer to that which will keep us working and strong. Is this how they think we are now in this country? Remember the new head of the environment said that we may have to create pollution and force it into the air to cool the earth down. Well aren't we doing that now and if we continue to do it and not put people out of work, wouldn't this country be in a better shape? *But aren't they just saying the opposite of what we have to do solve the problem now?* Stop driving, stop producing electric power with coal, and so on, wouldn't do the same if we kept doing it? But they know we ain't too bright because they continue to lie to us. So why are we killing our number one industry, putting people out of work just the way we are doing something to protect us from harm that has not happened.

They know we ain't too bright because we listen to them.

To keep the auto industry why don't we just do this? Knowing what we truly know about carbon di-oxide why don't we just stay with the standards we have now and say by 2020 that all major cities will be set up to have electric car hook-up. The industry keeps growing, a new division of each car company comes up, a new business of setting up the hook-up and everyone can still drive the gas and diesel vehicle but the carbon di-oxide footprint gets smaller. Common sense. The sad part of this is that the people of car producing states vote themselves out of a job or a cut in salary which ain't too bright. You can see they never heard a word he said, they just listen to words and promises not kept. I didn't cut job or salary but I believe in America and not the lies told to us because I can read and hear what people say.

Now the auto industry could have and still can just use common sense to help save itself.

Why don't the employees get a loan and just buy the companies. The best companies in this country and the ones that treat their employees the best are employee-owned. The vehicle coming out would be better because of the new pride that would go into it; now they'd have say in everything. Baldridge, at its best (a business theory that works) which most companies believe in. I just put thousands of hard-working men and women back to work and guess what, I haven't spent a dime of your money. They could get a loan from a major bank and pay them back. I'd bet you right now that Americans would get behind them because they also believe in the hard- working Americans in the auto industry. Again why rush to jump in without looking for other answers. We ain't too bright; it's about control. I just built up the jobs, economy didn't spend a dime. I let the bad banks restructure and have a chance to come back up with good leadership. Our economy would have never taken the big hits it just did. Yes, some of us would have lost money, but we would have put our grand- kids in debt just because no one wants to take the time to think about the true outcome.

—

Question: How many of our congressmen really read the spending bills before they pass them?

There are so many jobs and industries we could create that would help clean up this country, cut the cost to Americans on material and help put Americans back to work, but if you did that then you couldn't control them. This is a book about starting to think and if we did that and change the powers in Washington for people that believed in America, we could return to a small central government and strong state government.

Question: How many states are on strong footing and who runs them? Most states are run by Rep. Governors. Take a look at just two. Alaska and South Carolina are not in trouble but how about Michigan and New York? They're taxing everything that are not tied down..

Remember earlier I said President Bush was a Democrat in Rep. clothing, just look at the bills and money he spent. I hope you're getting the picture or are we just not that bright.

Another question I have, don't Americans have the right to work without having to pay for that right? So why are we as Americans, having to supporting unions and are trying to take away the secret ballot? Or better yet why are unions supporting them when they just put them out of work because of lies. To your surprise I am and have been a Union member. I have been president of my local and got the right to bargain with the employers. But what is hard to understand is when the union came in to help tell us how to bargain, they told the people on the bargaining committee that they didn't have to tell the members anything but everything is going all right. To me they didn't represent those people and they have a right to tell the people bargaining committee what they want not the other way around. All the union wanted was the memberships and the money, so I quit.

Here's my question to union bosses. Why not put the money you spend to buy politicians into education? Common sense! You are now building a work force to replace the retiring work force. They will be come out of high schools and colleges going to work on union jobs and your membership will grow by 10 times in a short period. But again that's common sense and not politics. The other thing union will gain from this is a better skilled worker because they over- see their development. Makes sense to me. Or just put the money in retirement plans and give the members a better shot at enjoying old age. Not spending it on liars who cost you your jobs. Or are we just not too bright?

Remember people do things out of fear. Most of the time not for the best reasons, just like the buyout; a bill was passed without anybody reading it and now we are paying for it for years or until we vote someone in who has common sense and is there for the people not the money. This last election was run on fear, hate and lies, not by the people but by the politicians and the main stream media thinking that we ain't too bright. They didn't care who they hurt as long as it put the money and votes on their side to remain in Washington. They'll divide and conquer with lies and hate because they know we ain't too bright.   So brighten up America, let's have real change next time we vote them all out and starting over with someone who's willing to fight for your right because they do represent you. Don't forget we are the government, not the people we elected and the constitution and bill of rights are what govern us.

And we are a republic with a small central government and a strong state government and that's too important to forget.

The Country and the World

Let's start with two questions. How many people think we should be part of a world government? What part has America played in the world that made us stand apart from the rest of the world? There are so many things, that I'd be writing for days. But here are just a few. The freedom to do what we want to do was given to us in the constitution. We have a Constitution and Bill of Rights that gave us this freedom. We believe that anyone can do what he needs to do to better them if they want. We believe in helping countries in need without asking for anything in return. We have come to the aid of counties in time of war. We are supposed to have a representative government but that's in question now. We have been the most productive country in the world until now. So why would someone hate this country?

America has always worked from strength and never from weakness like now. We always come to the aid of any country fighting for freedom and human rights. We now have our leaders going around the world saying what a bad country this is. If we're so bad why does everyone want to come to this country? We have fed the world at one time but our government has put a stop to that. Americans have been there for people in disasters with medical aid, food and equipment. How are we a bad country? If you don't love it, leave it was the saying in the sixties, but now it seems to blame our country for what is happening in the world.

When will the politicians realize you can't buy friends? We poured billions into other countries in time of need and then they turn on us. They have no clue as to what to do in Washington D.C., do they? When are our leaders going to understand what America is about and act like Americans,

---

44

and like we belong to the world but as a sovereign nation on to itself and take pride in this country? Yes we have made mistakes but we have done a lot of things right that helped other countries all around the world. Being sorry isn't going to change the past, but looking forward without jumping into things without doing the true research would. These politicians have got to stop blaming us for the past and start looking at the future. You learn (well some people learn, government can't seem to) from the past and don't make the same mistakes again but ours seems to want to make the same mistake. If you read about the past you learn what not to do. Or does our government want to make the same mistake for another reason. Dealing from weakness never gets the problems solved. Have you ever been in an area where you have to fight just to get by someone on the street? If you show strength things change for the better but weakness will get you nowhere. Most of our leaders have never been there have they, so how are they to know? Theory: It works for them. In history only the strong survey, nothing changed and it never will. Because of our greatness other countries came to us for help, now we are going to other countries to bail us out. What happened? It's called politics and politicians that's what happened. We just ain't too bright.

Let's take a look at what's happening in this country right now and you answer your own questions. Of course I'll ask a few also. We have 250 major cities in the country now fighting a drug war. The criminals from a third world country are over running our streets with drug, murder, and crime. Where has our government and law enforcement been? Handing out seat- belt tickets because of lack of funding to fight the drug war? States, cities and the federal government has failed to stop the flow of drugs because of weak laws and weak punishment for drug crimes. They have spent billions on the war with no good results. Most criminals in the drug business now are illegal aliens that come and go as they please. Our government refuses to close the border. Why? Because they are now slaves to the Democratic Party and vote without know what they voted for. Just ask Speaker Pelosi. Why hasn't our government done what is right for the country? Wouldn't stopping the illegal aliens from coming into this country help in slowing down the crimes? They have no fear of our laws because they know we have no backbone to control them. You ever wondered why? How about the fact that the Speaker of the house is telling the illegal immigrates to have no fear, for the government will not enforce their own laws on you. Why not, we want to add to our voting class even if it means your job going to them. How is that for a reason? Why would the third person in line for the presidency tell people from a foreign country to have no fear and go ahead and break our laws? (There is view tape of this) The state she represents is going bankrupt because of the illegal aliens' welfare, criminal system and legal expenses paying for the illegal aliens. Most people in her state think she represents them. Doesn't she care that she represents Americans and not aliens, who are now fighting to keep their heads above water in paying their bills and taxes. Or are they just not that bright. If you notice the last two statements had to do with how illegal aliens affect this country nationwide and the government refuses to act on it, while you are footing the bill. Why not, the Democratic Party needs votes; we are a world country, no longer a solvent nation on to ourselves, are we? Just ask Washington liberals. Is this what you wanted?

Have they forgotten what an Oath of Office means? Have they forgotten what our forefathers wanted for this country? Seems like they have but that's okay they can use words just words and promises just promises and they got us eating out of their hands. A Republic nation, with a small central and strong state government but thanks to California and many other states we are giving our powers to the federal government which was never supposed to happen. I know they have forgotten our Constitution and Bill of Rights just by their action lately, forming an elite government... so wake up Americans. If you read newspapers from overseas or watch news from there you can see how dumb they now think we are. The only thing you hear from Washington is Americans have spoken. Well didn't they speak with the Tea Parties and the election in Calif.? Or do they just listen when it's in the favor? When they had the tea parties those weren't Americans because they didn't tell congress what they wanted to hear. Here's a question for you. Why for the last two years under the Bush presidency didn't they do anything? Now that they are in power they are spending money they don't have, taking over companies and trying to control us at every turn of our lives. They only had a 9% rating and they are the same politicians. What has changed? The only thing is who has control off the Money and power.

Do you ever wonder why NBC, which is owned by GE, is always covering the President and his party so nicely? Well you know that is a big electric power contract that they want? What better way to get it then to pay to play. Conflict of interest or what? You'll never hear this from the main stream media, oh, I forgot NBC is the main stream media; I'd keep it quiet to. You can find out all this in congressional records.

By giving up what kept us safe, the methods used to gain information was an action taken after 9/11 to protect us. Both parties knew what was going on. By cutting our military budget and by working from weakness and hiding our heads in the sand about the truth, is this what's going to protect us? What's their plan for once the strongest nation in the world, and now everyone owns us. Thank the politicians for that. It's not about the parties now it's about standing up for America and the freedom we once had. If the government really wanted to pass good immigration laws use common sense. Here's how you do it. First put up new ports of entry that are set up to handle immigrants who have skills and want to come to this country to work and become working citizens, not just voters. They fill out the paper work with their job skills and what else they are willing to do for work. Find companies on this side of the border that needs them; issue them a tax no. to pay taxes. Make sure the companies have insurance for them and their families, housing and an educational system that can meet their needs. After five years without breaking our laws they can now become citizens. The only family they can bring over at first is just the wife and kids and that's it. This way there are no welfare cases which are breaking some states' back. Everything is taken care of.

For people in this country now all they have to do is sign up, go back home for a short time to make sure they have no criminal record, the companies will hold their jobs and they can become citizens. If they don't and get caught here they lose all rights to becoming an American citizen. From here on out if caught here without papers they get finger printed and sent back. Our Government will carry ads on all news media and Mexico will do the same for six months, now both sides cover it. There are other things you'll have to do but you can see how common sense can solve a lot of problems.

Staying with government control, why would a government even think of signing a treaty where the UN comes in and tells Americans how to raise their children? Does our government believe we are that dumb we cannot raise our kids? Well, yes they do, they been telling us for years now and take a look at the results. Ain't a pretty picture is it? The government thinks that Americans ain't too bright. They think they can lay their way into controlling us and we have let them. Remember at the start of this there is a page of Thomas Jefferson and it states the government should fear the public because if you fear the government we are no longer free. Ask yourself where we are at now. *all Americans, not just democratic and republican, but all Americans should think about this and send a message to our politicians, we are the government and you represent us, not the party, lobbyist, special interest, people with money, not foreign governments, but the people who elected you, not your ideals but us, we the people.* Remember lies, words and promises that were never kept this early in a new term? It's alright to like someone but when his signing a bill that no one read, is destroying our country by driving it into the poor house, and it spends money they don't have it's time to say *no more spending.* Let's use the term limits our forefathers gave us every 2-4-6 years and *vote the ones that don't represent the people that voted them in.* Only this, hear what they say not what is written for them to say. Take a look at their voting record and their lies, and then make the call. *Debt, fear or freedom. Your choice.*

VOTE

IT'S TIME FOR A REALITY CHECK. WHY IS OUR EDUCATIONAL SYSTEM FAILING?

As I look around at the school I teach in and watch as we fail to see or meet the needs of the students we are dealing with, I realize that it's time someone told the truth and not the lies our politicians and administrators want you to hear. Education is a big business and companies make big money from it. But yet we all know it's failing in this country. We all ask "Why?" But no one sees that the ones answering the question are the same ones creating the problems.

Who am I to say something like that? What do we know? Well I've been in education for twenty years now at all levels. The others are experts in the field. How can I compare to them. Maybe because they ain't too bright, about education and what really needs to be done, are they? If they are experts, why are we failing? Has anyone looked at that question? I was always told an expert is someone who could solve the problem and make it work. Where have they gone wrong? They failed to make it work and yet we listen to them. Ask 90% of teachers and they'll tell you *no child left behind is the biggest joke in education.* But the government who has no clue and isn't too bright about education, passed a bill they had no reason to pass. But because of lobbyist control congress they did and now education is even fighting harder to be successful with less money and lower standards.

Twenty years of working in education you get a chance to see firsthand how poorly education is run. But we ain't too bright. If you look at it from the employer's needs and what students want is totally different than what the government wants out of education. Because government only controls public education and has no say in private, you can compare and really see the difference, which we'll do later. Money is misspent because of government mandates and lack of knowledge of what really goes on in education. School districts and state department of education could save millions of dollars every year if they ran education like a business and for political gains, or as not something that is just there to babysit students until they get out of school.

The one thing I found and probably the most important thing is that government and administrators can't read the data. You'll see this many times in this chapter. Here is the data written about in Time Magazine and Newsweek in 1995 comparing public education to private education. 75% of students in public education do not want to go to college for many reasons which we cover later. In private education 95% go to college and 91% graduate. Why the big difference? Why are private schools more successful?

I came into education from the field where you have to be successful to stay in business but public education is federally funded. Now we all know the government can spend all they want on anything they want, so why worry about money? They can always go to the taxpayer for more money can't they, as has been proven time and time again? In the field businesses wants employees with work skills and good work habits but they are not getting them out of schools any more. Why? I was an employer so I know students have no work skills coming out of high school. Education is failing because of the way we teach now-a-days. We are forced to work as baby-sitters and not as teachers. We have lowered our standards to meet the NCLB which we should never have done.

In 1995 there was an article by Intel in the Seattle paper about how they had 4000 openings in a plant. 4000 people were asked to take the entry test. 20 % passed. What was the test made up of? It was geared to the ninth-grade level. Who took the test? College and high school graduates who went all the way in a failing system and not being able to pass a ninth grade test. If that doesn't show how badly we are failing, nothing will. 80% failed. They've gone all the way in a system that churns out poor results. If I were in business I'd be worried too. So how can you blame companies to want to hang on to employees even if they can't do the job? It'll cost them more to train a new person to help them fail than the bonuses. Same in education, it's better to have a warm body there than nothing. Here it is twelve years later and things are only worse. Why? Why are we still in this free fall in education? Why hasn't the government fixed it? We all know that the government only backs failures, so why should they care? Or why should we care, it's only our children's future, and the future of the country. Just throw more money at it and it'll go way until the next election, then we can make more promises and tell more lies about what we are going to do. But we ain't too bright, are we?

In 1990 when I started teaching, I was asked to help write the curriculum for the state of Idaho in Industrial Mechanics. The board was made up of businessmen from all major companies in the northwest, along with teachers. We sat down and wrote a curriculum to meet both the needs of business and education in all areas. Ideal,right? Try to take it back to administrators in education. They'll tell you that's not what they want; all students should go to college. Not too bright are they, because this is what would get them to college. Being able to pass a ninth grade level test would be a good start.

Being able to read data would help too. The reason 75% of students going to public do not want to go to college is, they ain't smart enough, wanting to go to work because they come from a broken home, no money and maybe they just want to do something else like be a welder, carpenter, plumber or something along that line or housewife, book-keeper, or cook all of which could be taught in high schools across the country. It was done in the 50s and 60s before the department was founded under Johnson. We now have a dying work force with no one to replace them because we took vocational education out of high schools. Do you ever wonder why the drop-out rate has gone up?

When you have students coming into high school not being able to read at a fourth-grade level, can't do the math at a sixth-grade level, what happens? The answer is easy. We talk about self-esteem but yet they have no idea how they feel when they have to compete with other students that can do this. So what's the first thing to do is look for a way out, because education doesn't see the problem. Going along these lines seven years ago at the school I was teaching in, the state department was running us down on what to do. Blame the teachers. But when asked to show us a school that had the same problems or a way to solve the problems, they told we were teachers and should be able to come up with an answer and they wanted to hear it the next time they came back. Remember these are PhD's. Masters of education and no answers! When they came back we presented a plan of putting all new students coming at these low levels into a two-hour block and work on these skills. We were told it wouldn't work so you're going to need a new idea. Seven years the same people came back and they found something to help solve our problem. Out in Calif. they have a new method of dealing with the problem and it was now going to cost the district 5000.00 a teacher to send them out to Calif. They were putting students coming in at low levels in reading and math in two- hour block and working with them to raise their levels. Someone didn't hear what we had said and now two things were going to happen. The district now has to pay for something we could have started seven years earlier without having to pay for and look at all the students we lost because someone wasn't too bright and couldn't hear.

The standards we have now couldn't get you by in the 60s and now you graduate. Teachers have now become baby-sitters because of the government and the legal system. Because if they made change that would raise the standards and made both the student and the parents accountable, they are afraid they'd get voted out. We ain't too bright are we? So here again the old saying, "if you want it to fail give it to the government" has real meaning.

Going back to the magazine article comparing public school with private school, the difference being who is held accountable. In private schools the administrators, teacher, parents and most of all the students are held accountable. Gee what an idea to hold the students accountable or the administrator and parents not just the teacher. It's always easier to blame the person at the bottom than anyone else. You can't fire parents, the administrators can fire a teacher and the student can blame this thing on everyone else. Why worry about the truth? Maybe this will explain why private school is successful and public schools aren't. Don't get me wrong, public schools are successful with a small group but that group will do well anywhere. But why do some many fail? Didn't President Obama just cut voucher to students in Washington D.C. and send them back to failing schools and this students were poor black kids from the hard part of D.C. Weren't most of them doing better and yet the government cuts their funding? Does that make sense? Not to me. Maybe prejudice, my guess.

Truth be known, the number one reason education is failing is because the government politicians and the administrators have no clue what's going on in the classroom and have no idea other than political answer which equals to throwing money at the problem. The second reason education is failing is because most of the administrator in charge couldn't cut it in the classroom, got an administrator's degree and put their failed ways in to school they run. Discipline has gone out of the window in education and the students and parents now run most schools. As you see our new President does not want our students looking at being the best, because being the best equals money but money is bad unless the government and the rich have the money. The third reason is no one wants to be accountable for what they do, from the administrator, parent, and the students who can all blame the teacher. Again, don't get me wrong we have a large amount of teachers who do their jobs well. But again it goes up hill, isn't the administrators in charge of the teachers and if the teachers are not doing their job who's supposed to straighten them out? If the students aren't following the rules set down, who is supposed to put them in line and who has the power to take actions? Not the teacher. Therefore our students are not afraid to fail.

Today because of the shortage of teachers, teachers can get by with doing as little as they can. Administrators don't go into classrooms to check on the teachers because they have many other meets. So how do you change this?

The best way is to pay good teachers better. How do you this? Common sense! If they maintain or raise the level of the students you pay them a bonus at the end of the year. Do a good job and get rewarded. Fail and get your regular pay. If you do it for five years you get a 5000.00 raise and still can work for your bonuses at the end of the year and repeat until they retire after 30 years in service. If you fail to do so you get put on a PDP after three years of poor performance. If no changes occur after two years, you are asked to go. Now administrators must go back into the classroom every five years and maintain the level or lose their administrative license: that way they will never forget what the job is about.

The other thing that has to be done is to look back at research project that was done by a professor in Oregon back in the 50s that proves just what needs to be done in education to meet the needs of the students. But as normal the government pulled its research when it proved to work. Here's the story covered by Sixty Minutes back in the nineties. The professor received a grant to study what going back to the basics would do in education. He went down to Mississippi where they believe blacks couldn't learn. He then went back to the basics and in 5 years the students in this project were out-performing the students in regular school. So what happened, they pulled the project and the grant and kept it quiet for years. Tell me government wants education to be successful. But we ain't too bright, are we?

What we need to do at the lower levels is go back to the basics and make sure every student can read and do the math. Meet the needs of Special

Ed in public schools but not take away from the students who don't have special needs. Keep computers and calculators out of the classrooms. Let them learn the formals and the hands-on skills. In the seventh-grade add the computer and the calculator in and now the students can pick up the speed but without the basics you have no speed. But this is only using common sense and the results would surprise you. Not me, but you, because I have believed in this for years.

Another thing we have to do is to get rid of what I call the *leeches*. Companies with political pull which sells the government garbage about education, make billions from the government, put money back into politician's re-election and get contracts that take money away from good project and sell garbage. Proof: At the school where I was at and needed restricting, along with many schools in the state, they brought in a company from back east who were selling Baldridge and PDSA (Plan, Do, Study, Act) which is nothing more than a lesson plan which is a Plan, Do, Study, Act. But they thought we weren't too bright but it covered the administration, state department, and the politicians who said they were going to make changes. Remember change isn't always for the good as proven here. It's like everything else like the going on in Washington. It makes money for someone but does nothing for the average Americans or education. If someone with common sense would look into the waste by education they find more money than they would ever need to make changes for the better. But of course not being too bright I forgot money is the answer to everything according to the government even if it takes it away from American family. The thing that really impressed me was when they had a teacher that believed in this new grading and education system in which the student can get the answer wrong but gets a better grade than the one that gets the right answer and does it the old and right way. How's that for making education better? Needless to tell you the old teachers were mad but who wants an educated public? Government doesn't. There is an old saying that goes like this, "An uneducated man will follow and only do as asked, but an educated man will ask why, who is it going to help, why is it this way, and in the long run will find out the truth." Which one are you? As the government and news media know, we are not too bright. If this is education at its best, I can now see why we are behind third world countries in science and math and who knows what else!

As I said earlier that the government doesn't know how to read data, here's more proof. President Obama is saying that government should take over all college loans. No more private loans or scholarships, or paying for college as you go but in return you must work for the government after you get educated in public service to help repay your loans. Can't any one read data in Washington or in education? Earlier I talked about the fact that 75% percent of students do not want to go to college, but what does that matter? Washington's going to tell you what they need you to do for them and not what you can do for yourself and owning the government has nothing do with controlling you, does it? Talk about taking over your life. *If the young people buy into this, our future is in the tank.* We better make sure we teach our children the Constitution and Bill of Rights before they buy into this educational system. Remember nothing comes for free so just how much are you willing to give them of your freedom? Again we are not looking at the true idea behind government college loans and working for the government for a few years. Try this on for size. How about by doing it this way we are now indoctrinating young people into the way of thinking that you work for the government and not as our forefathers wanted it. The government works for you, what an idea; I think communism ran on the same idea. Gee, is Collin Powell thinking, didn't he fight against communism as a general. I will tell you later. But again we're not too bright.

What is a teacher's job? Their job is to educate students on how to get by in life with basic job skills like reading, writing and math. They can also help them find an area that they are interested in and show them how to reach them with the skills they've learnt in high school. Let's raise the standards, not lower them and get our educational system back where it belongs, on *top*. Unlike, where our leadership is taking us, to the bottom, not the top. In their eyes everyone should get an *A* without working for it. I'm not going to cover everything that needs to be done because this is a book on how our government is failing us by going away from what our founding fathers believed in. But we're not too bright, we are just buying into everything they are selling and losing everything our forefathers gave us, freedom of choice, liberty and rights which are now being taken away by backdoor laws, like global warming, green laws and so on.

The thing people should look at is this fact. Education is *political*. So they hire people with papers and political pull and not people who can get the job done. They have PhD's, Master's degrees but that doesn't mean they can get the job done.   It's like going to a horse sell, you look at the papers but it doesn't always mean they can get the job done, does it? Just look at the horse that just won the Kentucky Derby, a $9000.00 dollar horse, against horses that cost millions and yet he won. He had the right training and could get the job done unlike our political appointments that only have the connections. Common sense not money should talk but no longer in this country and our politicians are selling us out. Education is no different from anything else. Money talks! But we ain't too bright are we!!

LET'S TALK

As you can see I'm basically asking questions you should be asking yourself, if you care about your future and this country's future. If the answers you come up with make you happy and they go along with the elected officials, and you really can't see the truth, we as Americans are in deep trouble. But along this line here are some more questions you should ask yourself. Do you believe in representative government? Do you believe in freedom of choice? Do you believe the government is working for you? Or do you believe you are working for the government? Do you believe in communism? Do you believe that the government has the right to tell just how your life should be lived? Don't get me wrong, I believe we need some laws but not on everything we do. Do you still believe the main stream media? Where can you find the true answer if the media lies to you? When you answer these questions along with the other questions and the question to come and see where you truly stand. Democrat, Independent, Republican or whatever party you belong to this what you elected them to do? Do you know what rights the Constitution and the Bills of Rights guarantee us and are willing to give them up for what's coming? Are we not that bright that we'd give them up? Hard questions, but easy answers if you believe in America, do you believe? Well, do you?

What happened to freedom of speech with the tea parties? The main stream media tried to make them look like just a bunch of angry people that are unhappy with the fact that we have a black president, or prejudice, or just not too bright Americans, so far from the truth. Again this goes back to divide and conquer. Just take a good look at the people who were there, blacks, whites, rich, poor, educated, common ordinary Americans who think the government is out of control with spending and trying to take the ideals our forefathers gave us. To Americans it was people speaking out for them because they can't. This didn't take place on a holiday, weekend or any other special day. They came together to say stop spending our money. Stop putting us and our future in debt for them to have power. It's so easy for them to lie to us anymore, isn't it? Do you really trust your elected officials in Washington D.C.?

Was the buyout needed? Why couldn't the oversight committees of both parties see what was to come? You know they did and they did nothing. 9% congress! Well what this book is written for is for you to ask yourself these questions and more. Come up some answers and take action in the next election or even now. If you think your elected official represents you, call them up and tell them what you want and see what happens. This will tell you who they represent, you or money and power? Hope for the best and we'll just see how bright you are. Here is what happens if you want to know and look up. The spending started under President Carter and carried on until now when everything came apart on them because the government refused to take actions. Why? Because it meant votes! Votes mean power and power means money. Point the finger at some else while you pull the wool over Americans' eyes. We just ain't too bright just like they think or know.

Why would a smart government back bad loans? Not too bright? If that's the answer why did we vote for them? We must not be too bright. Aren't our elected officials supposed to be bright? If that's the case what happened? I covered it earlier and how there was an attempt to get things done but congress and parties refused to act. Who do we blame, them, or us for voting them back in? Why were large banks forced by the government to make bad loans even if they knew they were not going to be able to make the payments? If you think you are smart and that I'm just playing, just do the research. It's easy just start with congressional records in the 70's under Carter. Why is Fanny and Freddie backed by the government and why did they buy up all these bad loans? Doesn't it make you wonder or are you like sheep and just follow? No business sense or better known as common sense or did they have another idea in mind? Things aren't just black and white are they? Why did members of both parties just jump in there and add pork to the buy- out? Again why didn't they read it? Do they just believe Americans don't care? So far they are right and the few that did show that they were angry with what was happening were called idiots by some in the media and other elites.

If you're listening and not hearing the truth and buying into everything, then we ain't too bright. The other thing is you haven't answered all my questions honestly. Why is it that we just sit back and let a few, say what we think? Are most Americans afraid to stand up; are we cult members, or do we just not care? Aren't you angry yet? The answer on how to solve the problems will, come, and it's so simple.

Remember we're just talking. Speaking of talking, why would anyone that represents Americans want the freedom of Information Act reinstated? What happened to freedom of choice? Shouldn't I have the right to listening to anything or anyone I want? Of course if they cut out everything but good country music and old time rock and roll from the fifties I'd agreed. But that's not what it's about. It's about silencing anyone who disagrees with them so we can't hear the other side or maybe even the truth. That's what they are afraid off, because maybe someday soon American's not Democrats or Republicans, but Americans will wake up and hopefully before it's not too late to do something.

Remember talk radio and the internet has kept things alive as far as the truth as to what is happening in this country today. Just as this book was written to challenge you and the elected politicians, so is talk radio and you silence them you silence the truth. We already made it hard for Americans to read because we haven't truly taught Americans how to read. If you remember I am a teacher so I'll put it to you as one of my students put it to me "Hitler burnt the books as we just don't teach the young how to read the books." Sad that came out of a high school student's idea of the government and education. Sometimes I think we do have a future with students thinking like this. But what will they have to pay to have the freedom we are now giving up before they can live the way we did.

If you look at the list of who the new leaders think are terrorists or future terrorists, you find that anyone who believes in the Constitution or Bill of Rights is one in their eyes. Look it up on the internet, it will surprise you. Here's just a few, military men returning from overseas duty, people who believe in gun rights, are against high taxes that believe we don't need big government, strong religious belief, just to name a few things that they look at to put you on this list. Funny isn't it that the things that were given to us by our forefathers now make us enemies of the state.

Funny thing is I love history and history tells many stories but my question is, why can't we learn from the past. Maybe because we just ain't too bright or maybe some of us can't read the truth in history and seeing how it repeats itself. Remember the big change in Russia in the 1900's, Germany in the 30s and countries losing their freedom now in the world we are living in? Read history and you'll see that we are going through the same thing here in this country. Unions and government took over companies in Russia in 1900's, before they fell into communism. Elite ruling class but all this came about with a war; here we are just giving it over. Here their doing it with words and action by our own government. All they do is pass bills, spend money and say we have a crisis and they can save us. We ain't too bright. Smooth talking and lies get it done here in America. In Connecticut gun control by just having someone say something and they take you guns away. The criminal still keeps their guns but the honest citizen loses them because somebody wants to get their guns. Or put insurances on guns no one can pay, you're breaking the law and they come and take them away, back doors tactics but we ain't too bright are we. You voted for these idiots. Taxes on ammo, registration of ammo, all back door tactics used for gun control. But if it becomes law now you are the criminal, and they can take you guns. How dumb are we? All you have to do is tell them not to pass these laws but will you? By voting them out and electing politicians who believe in a constitutional government. Even if you just read what has happened before and the freedom of individuals has been lost. Is that what you want? Who is the government, the elected or the people of this country? Think about that before the next election, if you have a choice by then.

Have you ever asked yourself why our forefathers gave us the right to bear arms? To form a Militia even if it's against our own leaders. Thomas Jefferson, whom President Obama likes to quote, said, "Sometimes government needs a cleaning out." They gave us that right to clean them out every election so why don't we use it next election and stop the wholesale of this country by the greedy elite in Washington who are pointing fingers at everyone but themselves.

If they care about Americans why then haven't they stopped the craziest going on in California? The silver minnows have cost 30 and can go as high as 80 thousand jobs in this area. Cutting our food supply in the most productive part of the country is only going to drive prices up when most families can't afford. It can also cost more jobs in other areas of the country. It'll also force us to go outside this country for food. Why? Who has paid them enough money to hurt Americans? When is a fish more important than jobs and people? Why are we pumping millions of gallons of water into the ocean instead of using it to help America? Why can't we do both? I know common sense would help but as we all know Washington only runs on money and election funding. The average hard-working man cannot give them that. So they end up paying with loss of jobs and homes because we can't put money in their pockets. If this were not true common sense would have told them to release the water for farming and why isn't the main stream media screaming for something to be done? When this book comes out something may have gotten done, but if not, you are in trouble. If only I could read! Where is the Yellow brick Road that leads to Oz? Cause this ain't America.

Again remember we are just talking. If you listen and read what the Spanish Politicians and Professors are saying about Cap and Trade in their country and they've been under it since the 1997, you ask yourself, why do we want that here? Because now our representative government thinks they know better. Why not, they only buy into failure so why not another one? Bio-fuel, failing if you do the research, costing billions, education, costing billions, and the list goes on. But what they are saying in their country is that it's costing one million Euros to create one job for the government while losing 2 and half jobs are lost in the private area. Hey, that's a great trade out, isn't it? Two jobs for the government, 3 people losing their jobs so that the government can get two jobs and the tax payers can pay for them with more taxes. Just ask our government. But the government does not produce a product so how can they get money? Print it or tax the working class or do both. But the elite don't have to worry, do they? They are losing companies to other countries because they cannot afford to stay in Spain; people go cold in the winter because they cannot pay their electric bill. But that's okay here because here we'll tax companies that move to other countries. What about the jobs lost? You can't tax them. But all is not lost for them, they have found a country that wants to buy what they tried and failed. I guess because they are not too bright and can't see what happens when all you want is control everything in different names like environment, or global warming or any other lie they think they can sell to a not so bright public. Remember what I said about reading and looking at history, well, here is a country that tried it and says it's a failure and yet our government wants you to believe that it can work with different results and everything tells them it can't. Talk about being arrogant or dumb no matter, they are one and the same.

Again remember President Obama wanted us to take a look at France. Why not? 75% of France's electric power comes from Nuclear, safety, clear and no way to tax it so that leaves it out here. You got to remember our politicians just hit us with a large debt that a common sense person can solve without the debt but Americans seem to like the lies and taxes.

Here's the problem, they know by now only a few Americans will react and they can be controlled by the media because most of the rest are not too bright or belong to their cult, so why worry?

Have you noticed how many foreigners are telling us not to buy into government run health? Do you ever wonder why? They are also telling us we have the greatest health system in the world, so don't change it. Because they come here for treatments their government will not pay for. We now have the best doctors in the world because of the system we have here. My question is why would you want to trade down to a failing system from a good system? American government loves failure. But us Americans like being the best and it's called pride. Mr. Obama and congress have no pride in being Americans; elected politicians should try it sometime. My friends from Canada tell me how dumb we'd be if we change our health system. The British have told us the same thing. I know our politicians aren't listening because that's not what they want to hear. So they make up their own lies. Our own doctors tell us it will cause problems but does anyone listen to them?

Again we are just talking. Why don't we stop Bio-fuel and just put the land back into farm production, raise a crop, drop the cost of food, sell the rest overseas and pay off our debt? Remember this is costing us billions just to keep these companies afloat so why not cut our losses in a time like this when we are spending money we don't have. Remember our credit cards are now saying no, but being the government we'll just print more money.

Start the promised drilling in this country, offshore and turn coal into gas and diesel. Put in the nuclear power plants like the rest of the world, if the government wants to be like the rest of the world. Keep the 700 billion from going overseas and start cutting into our debt. This was one of the things that G.W. Bush did, so if they did not like G.W., why not become oil independent like Americans want? But not our congress, they just took two millions of acres of prime oil reserve off the list and all because of environmental protections. Get smart, the only thing we have to protect our environment from is the government and the large pocket books of people who have no clue as to what the environment needs. To them we live in Oz. Control and lies. Cost would go down on both products or you can believe the liars in Washington and the lobbyists who make a killing of buying and selling our congressmen and women. Why didn't we just let the car companies go bankrupt? How can a union own a business when are there to protect the employees from the evil, greedy, money- hungry employers? Who are they going to fight now for higher wages? Themselves! What is wrong with this picture? How come unions got a 100% and creditors only 29% and why were pushed around by the President and his people? Why didn't they just sell it to the employees, give them a loan and let them run it. Because if they did that, they'd have no control and it had a chance of becoming successful and they had to show government power over Americans. It's not about saving a company, it's about power. Not only that, if they sold it to the employees, they might have paid it back and the government would be out of it. No control of a company to who will be forced to build junk for cars.

What if we didn't have the buy-out and let the companies go under? It's like the government, they have mismanagement but no one takes responsibility for it. So why buy them out? Well, if you really follow the money you'll see just how government and big business are in bed together along with unions and the ones that pay needed to get paid back for backing the politicians. Yes a lot of us would lose money. I know I did, but in the long run we'd have come out ahead but no one is going to tell you that. Just refer back in this book as to who's coming out ahead? Did you know the economy is coming back slowly and the government has only used 4% of the money set aside? What's wrong with this picture? Remember mismanagement causes business to fail, isn't our government failing because of mismanagement? The carbon di-oxide footprint is not what we have to fear, it's the lack of common sense when it comes to dealing with it. The thing that surprised me is the fact that the older people fell for the lies because back in the 50s we were supposed to freeze to death by the year 2000. But I guess it's easier to sell warming then freezing to death because the freezing cycle just didn't cooperate like a little heat. Half a degree in a hundred year is something really to fear? But now Al Gore and his mini-minds are getting caught in their own lies and the profit he has made by selling his lies is catching up with him. So the government has got to act quickly on this before the next crisis they create comes along. As Mr. Gore say "he is putting his money where his mouth is." My question is, why do we have to put our money there? He's gotten rich off you. But again we are not too bright.

Wasn't talking fun? But remember what our forefathers wanted for us and how they gave it to us. They gave their blood in many wars, love and pride for this country and all you hear from our leaders is what a sorry

---

country we now live in. We made the world a better place in many ways but in their eyes we as Americans do not desire of what they died for. How could politicians like this be elected? Love or leave again was the saying in the sixties, what happened? Freedom, of choice, right to work, right to pursue happiness, right to bear arms, freedom of speech, small central government, strong state government. Why are we so willing to let them go? For words just words and promises just promises and lies, just lies just for their greed for power and money. They lived it and fought to give us the way of life we have known for two centuries and now are we just going to give it away? Why does our government always play on fear? The sky is not falling, the ocean not filling up, but hate and prejudice is coming back because of our government and trying to divide Americans and throw out one of the key things this country was founded on. The belief in God and his helping hand that guided the founding fathers. Yes, this country is in trouble but not from the problems that can be fixed with common sense but the government within. Karl Marx wrote the Communism Manifesto in the early 1900's and said that the mighty country of America would destroy itself from within. How right he was!

WHAT'S WRONG WITH THIS PICTURE?

If you look around you see a lot of things that don't make sense but we just call what's wrong with this picture. The reason I called this chapter this, is because of a picture I saw in the New York Times of the Statue of Liberty with a whip. What's wrong with this picture? Who drew it? Why would a big time Newspaper and a person that draws (I wouldn't call this art and I wouldn't call him an artist) have so little respect for this country, its symbol of Freedom given to us by the France? Why has all this come about since the last election and the new leadership in this country? We used to have pride in this country, but since they have been going around the world running this country down it seems that it's ok for everyone to do it. If I was getting that paper it is dropped in a heartbeat for something that low. I'm an American who still has pride in this country but where are the rest of the Americans that had the same pride?

What's wrong with this picture that we now look down on this country? I can't see anyone having a reason to do so unless you look at our leadership. You'll see a lot of things wrong with these pictures. It doesn't matter whether you are a Democrat, Republican or an Independent, you got to draw the line somewhere and say enough is enough. Our leadership is not leading us in the right direction. When you start running down the country that gives you the right to represent Americans in a free election and now you're trying to destroy what our forefathers give us. Take a hard look at this picture and tell me what's wrong with it. We are not too bright, are we?

What's wrong with the picture that makes me ask these questions? You answer them. Tell me why our representatives lie to us on a regular basis and think we are too dumb to tell when they are lying? Tell me about how they are driving us into debt that we don't need? Tell me how everything now is a crisis and we don't have the time to do the research to solve the problem with common sense and get it done without spending billions? Tell me just how we got to this point in our country where we are now, the enemy of the state, if we believe the way our forefathers did? What's wrong with this picture when if we believe in freedom of choice, freedom of speech, the second amendment, no gun control, return as a soldier from overseas duty you are now someone who can become the enemy of the state? What's wrong with this picture when someone who was willing to give his or her life for this country, comes home is now going to stop believing in this country? Try this on for size. The government is afraid of them now because they have the training to stand up to a corrupt government and if you're trying to destroy what they fought for, you know they are not going to support you, are they? Like they did in the election they make you the enemy or the bad guy. So what's wrong with the pictures they printed of the Governor Palin? The evil witch from the north! Well that's just it, they printed the picture in the lying news media and they are still doing it. Why are they so afraid of her? The truth be known, is because she is America, and if Americans wake up and see through the words just words and the promises just promises and the lies, maybe they'd find out just what they had missed. Remember she would have sat over the senate and where do we have a lot of corruption with politicians with bad dealing? Would you want someone who fights corruption in her party watching over you, knowing she will point you out for not doing your job? Not really.

Why hasn't the news media printed the same picture of Pelosi who has many bad pictures to print as the evil witch of the south? What's wrong with this picture and I can get pictures and video of this where Pelosi told illegal immigrants that we should stop all raid on them. They are breaking our laws and its okay? What's wrong with this picture when she took an oath to protect our laws? What's wrong with this picture where she told Americans she had no knowledge of the things that went on in Gitmo when she was briefed and it's on congressional record? What's wrong with this picture when the person third in line from being president feels she can lie to the American people any time it suits her needs and goes out and tells it's okay to break our laws and other congressmen back her? What's wrong with this picture if the main stream media covers up for all these lies and misdeeds?

Staying in California: What's wrong with this picture when their senator stands up and says "85% of the people that voted for me, told not to vote for this bill (first buy out bill) but I am going to vote for it?" Well, first of all wasn't she elected to represent their wishes? Second, why would she go against their wishes? Maybe she doesn't represent them but the party and the money that got her elected and not the people that voted her in to represent them. Yes, Mrs. Finstein, you were voted in to represent the people who voted for you but yet you voted against them. Why? Who do you represent if not them? Who put you there or was it the money? But like most Americans I'm not too bright so explain it to them and me. Add in plenty of lies just so we can feel right at home with you, but not too bright. You see represent means to represent the constituency who elected you, not the party or money. But forgive me, this is the new government we voted in, after all we ain't too bright because we all know they don't represent the people but who put the money to get them there.

This just touches the surface of what goes on in Washington and yet we sent them back. Again we ain't too bright are we? But what's wrong with this picture? The Sec. of Treasury did not pay his taxes as did many of the new people in the government. But when appointed he did. What a surprise he owned taxes but it was an oversight. Now let's take a look at an average citizen who didn't pay $2000.00 dollars in taxes. They filed a lien against his wages, froze his bank account and threatened to put him in jail, all for $2000.00. What action was taken against all these people who were in the six figures? They get appointed high offices in the new government. How about discrimination for starters? But that's politics and if you are high up or got connections, you can break the law and get a good government job. Wow! If I'd of know that I would never have paid my taxes and I could now have a high-paying job with great retirement benefits, boy did I blow it! As you guessed it was me that owned that $2000.00 and that's what happens to me. But Americans going through hard times sometimes have to do things to get by and we did get by. So what's wrong with the picture and all the appointments that didn't pay their taxes on time?

As you may or may not know we have a lot of elected officials on the wrong side of law in Washington D.C. but yet they get elected. People in their states ain't too bright because if they can break the law and cover it up just to stay in Washington, do you think they care about the people they are supposed to represent? What's wrong with this picture? What is wrong with this picture is that corruption is showing its face in Washington and

Americans are no longer outraged. Have we stopped caring for our freedom just to be taken away by the government? Why don't we start hearing what they are saying instead of just listening?

What's wrong with this picture when a President that says he is a Christian goes to a Catholic college and has a picture of Christ covered up? What's wrong with this picture when he represents a country that was founded with God and the belief in God written all over the founding father papers and tells the world we are not a Christian country? What country does he represent because it's sure not this one? Where are the Christians in this country who forsack their religion and voted him in, not questioning his action? What's wrong with this picture when he blame us for the problems of the world? Well, because of happenings in this country in the last six month, he can. What's wrong with this picture that the President of the United States can have companies in this country taken over with no worries about the outcome?

What's wrong with this picture that a person running for office in one state only has $5000.00 from the people of his state and $600,000.00 from outside interest? Who do they represent because this is happening nationwide? What's wrong with this picture that candidates are now getting funds from companies outside the states that have a vested interest in the state? Pay to play is what it's called. What's wrong with this picture that people of these states are not voting them out. Don't worry its happening in both parties. *Wake up America before it's too late.*

These are just a few of what's wrong with this picture issue we now face. But who's not covering these issues? Like what's wrong with this picture that this new budget spends more money in one budget than all the other budgets in the history of this country put together. Are we just that dumb or are we just having everything come at us so fast we don't have time to really get mad because we don't know how to react? Why don't you as Americans put a list of what's wrong with this picture for yourself and see what you come up with because this book is set up to be a wake-up call before the next election-cycle.

What's wrong with this picture? They just had a banquet in Washington D.C. for the press and the highly elite people and with President Obama. Hollywood actors, top press people, the rich, and how many middle-class working people did you see? Has anyone figured it out that these are the people who put him where he is today? Has anyone figured it out that he gives us lip-service, represents the people who can give him money to get to this office? Does he realize that not one of these people understand what the middle-class is, jobs losing, losing home, middle class is going through while they dress up in high-dollar cloth and eat high on the hog. This is a kick in the teeth to middle-class Americans. The only other time I even heard of something like this was when my brother-in-law went to Russia. They showed him a great time while outside he also saw the bread lines and the hardships and sufferings of the working man. But you got to remember they have a right to, for he's not the first president to do this, is he? You can't blame him for just doing what has been set there for him to take advantage off. We let them do it and ask only that they look good doing it. *We ain't too bright are we?*

They are forming an elite group of people who will run this country into the ground and if they get it done they will not worry about the average American, sorry to say. But this is only a book and my opinion. Pray they prove me wrong for the sake of our kids and grand-kids.

What If?

What if this book was to come to an end?   What if you hadn't read this book? Would you still think the same? What if you feel you now can make a change if you just take part in your government by voting? What if I could show you a government that would work for you? Would you remain a cult member and follow the party? Would you rethink the way you feel and vote a new leadership in? What if this was a bad dream? It ain't and you have to wake up and become part of the answer not a part of the problem.

A lot of what ifs ain't there? What if you had people and a government that worked for everyone and not just the rich and powerful? If I learned anything from watching the News and President's party is that money, power and an elite group have no sense of honesty. They don't care who and how they attack people that have opposing views. It's our way or we'll tear you apart and you can't do the same to us because we're in power now. What if they really cared about Americans and America, do you think they would think that way? Sad, isn't it, that opposing views are now just something to joke about? Well, if you want to change the change that is driving this country into bad times just *vote* in the next election. So what if everyone really votes what they want for this country, what would we see? Remember this is the *What If* chapter.

So let's start off with what if *all* Americans did take part in the government? What if you had a true American say "I'm running for President and here's how I'll straighten out the government and the country." Start off with no more lies, here's what I need from you. If you believe in me, there are two things I need from you. The first thing is your signature on a petition to get me on the Presidential list and second $100.00 for the election campaign. With those hundred dollars you just brought your first politician. If 50 million believe and donate I'd be the cheapest president to be bought in the last few elections and Americans would be who I represent. Not big money, lobbyist or special interest groups who invest millions into both parties to make sure they have a say in government dealing with issues that they need taken care of. He'd represent just the Americans who can't buy politicians or depend upon them to do what's right for America and the citizens that live here.

He belongs to no party, as you see he owes no one but Americans special treatment. The job he wants is to be President of the once greatest nation and return it to its one time greatest. Not to tear it down to be like any other country but to be respected for doing the right thing for the right reason. Not for money and power and fame. But a person (man or woman) who believes in the hard-working Americans, in this country and the things that made America great. One who believes that Americans can become and do what they want as long as it's right for America. What if that person believed in common sense and not fears and lies to get things done? What if he didn't believe in a large government like our forefathers did back then? What if that person didn't think government and election should be dependent on officials being brought and paid for by big money, special interest, no lies and not money but the Americans?

Yes money makes the world go round but it shouldn't make our government. This is a government founded on a government for the people and by the people not for the money, lobbyists, and special interest groups with money. How much politicians have forgotten about what this country was founded on? But if you want power and control you must forget. What if that person won, now you could change the election system as far as raising money and putting it back in the voters hand not the moneys hands? How's that for what ifs?

Here's how you put Americans back to work without spending their money to do it. Let you know right up front that there is no global warming unlike this administration which is just changing the name and creating another area of fear with same outcome to control of your life. Global warming was done for greed and money and Al Gore just said that in not so many words. So now they have to throw him under the bus and change the point of attack for the same results. Just like in the 50s when we had global freezing but that was hard to sell and the weather didn't change to back up their lies just like it hasn't changed to meet their new lies on warming.

—

Start drilling off shore, drill here, put coal into refineries to cut the cost of fuel. Keep the standards in place to keep the auto industry going without any more buy-outs. Become oil independent and stop sending our money overseas. Help start companies at looking at building electric cars and have them ready by 2020 for all major cities. Stop producing bio-fuels and start producing crops that we can sell overseas, therefore dropping the cost of food in this country. Restart our manufacturing industry and bring it back here because we need the jobs and use our great brains to bring the pollution down.

We talked about it before but carbon di-oxide is not our enemy, the government has just told you or that by naming people like soldiers coming home from overseas, or people who believe in religion and the Constitution, things like that. Remember carbon di-oxide is taken in by plants to grow and turn out oxygen, the thing that gives us life. Amazing how things become life-savers once the truth comes out and not the lies. But of course you have to do the research which government has a hard time finding the time to do things like read a bill for billions of dollars before they sign it. All it had to do was just be written by congress and that as good as taxpayers income, for taxes to pay the bills they couldn't read. First of all, you got to understand fear and lies make great reason for writing bad bills. The reason people buy into lies is because they repeat it enough in news and speeches that before the true research is done they already do the damage in bad bills, taking your freedom away and putting Americans out of work. When is President Obama going to stop campaigning and start doing the job he was elected to do, which is to truly act in the best interest of the Americans and not that of the parties. He is a great spokes-person but we elected him President not someone to go around the country as a spokesperson.

There is an e-mail going around asking NFL or NBA. Talks about all the laws, drug, felonies, wife beating, DWI, that have happened in the last year. So which one was the winner? Neither, it was your congress. What a sorry note for us if that's what we voted in to use common sense and honesty. How many congressmen and women have been caught in lies, mostly Democrats, how many people have broken major laws in this country and took an oath to defend our laws? And yet we send them back to represent us. The elite only want to represent the elite because they have the money. That's why we need somebody from the working class to represent us. You'll never get it unless you stop listening to the parties and start looking for someone the wants to give up their life for this country. Can you just think of the battles they'd have to fight if you don't elect other politicians to fight the same battles with them?

I figured out what politically correct means, never point out the truth if it exposes politicians for the liars they are or if can come back and bite you. Then you don't point it out. That's politics around the world unless you are a dictator. Then you just throw them in jail. Remember I use common sense. The thing is, it's a party that set the standards they run on, not the person.

The biggest problem we have now is that the young people don't read. They don't understand just what's happening to them since the last election. They can't find jobs and their future is in debt to the government because of this congress which they don't need. But the sad part of it is they wouldn't know what hit them until it's too late to do something about it if they don't wake up. What if they woke up and saw the truth? What if they heard the truth and could see a better future that they might miss out on if they don't wake up and vote in the next election? What if they said it's time to take their future back by voting out corrupt government? What if they realize all they have to do to prove they are the government, is just vote.

What if the Republican Party or the Independents were smart enough to realize that if they had someone running against President Obama to challenge him on all the spending, the lies and corruption, This would give Americans something to compare to that if they used common sense we could put Americans back to work, save homes and cut the future debt by repeating the unread bill that was passed. Now he'd have to come up with better reasoning and not along party lines.

What if we had people without party ties running for office? What if they were telling the truth and not the lies we now hear from our politicians? What if they cared about building this country up and not tearing it down? What if we didn't pass laws to protect us from ourselves that go against the Constitution and the Bill of Rights? What if they didn't use fear tactics and lies to gain control of us? *What if special interest, lobbyists, and people with money couldn't buy our politicians to pass laws that are only for special interests and special issues?*

What if they worked for Americans? But until we as Americans started looking for people who don't want power and money, have common sense, and care about Americans, will we have change. What runs congress now?

Example: Dodd took $5000.00 from in state, $600,000.00 from out of state interest, who is he working for? Is he for the money or the people of the state? You answer the question with truth in mind.

73

What if we really had a *government for the people by the people, not for the rich or elite?* What if everyone could reach their goals and reach their dreams without the government coming in the way. The bigger the government gets, the more the corruption will come in. *Government should fear the people, but when people fear the government you are no longer free.*

Are we now free or do we honestly fear the government is my question to all Americans who wanted change?

What if our leaders kept their Oath and protected our Constitution and protected our laws for America and Americans? *Sorry America!* That's not going to happen as long as we have the elected officials. We have now a 9% rating not because they wanted the government in office to do good, but because they wanted them to fail so they could take over, step in and pull the wool over eyes like they did. A lot of what ifs, but do you want real change for the better, than ask the question to yourself and your elected officials. California just told their state officials no more out of control spending. We live on our means and it's hard enough. Stop making it harder for us by putting us in debt and our kids in debt for your corruption.

WE THE PEOPLE

How we the people can take our government and country back from the corruption we now have in place in Washington D.C.

Our founding fathers gave us a way to stop things like this. Elections and term limits. Yes, term limits, two yrs., four yrs., six. And if they don't do the job, vote them out. How many times have we sent the same person back and get the same results? Yet we refuse to vote them out. But we the people have got to be smart enough to see what is happening when we send them back and we aren't. The meaning of the word insanity is doing the same thing over and over and over again, only expecting different results, it's the same results over and over again. We're getting the same results and we vote the same bought and paid for people in and expect something different and we're not getting different results, it's the same results over and over again and we send them back to Washington. The only way it's going to change is when the Americans wise up and change who we send to represent us. Not the bought and paid for people, or hand-picked people by the parties, or people who can raise money, but people who will represent the people who elected them. We are not going to get that until we the people are willing to put our money where mouth is.

We had an election last Nov. for people to go back to Washington D.C. to stop the health care act from coming in, what did they do? Fund it. Stop the illegal immigration. What did these elected people do? Fund it. Basically the ruling class in Washington pulled the new people aside and told them we got you here (not the people who elected them) but the party did and now you're going to pay us back by voting

—
75

the way we tell you to. They're not elected by the people in Washington, they are elected by the people of the state to represent them and their wishes, not the parties, special interest but the people of the state.

But when you have people like Newt Gingrich say that these people are elected to go back and make their choice, and not represent the people who elected, they should be voted out.

This is a representative government, who but who do they represent? Not the American people, but the people who buy them. Why are we not smart enough to see that? We are blinded by the words, just words, the promise, just promise, lies, just lies. If Americans aren't willing to change that, they better understand that they will have to put money where their mouth is to find a candidate that is interested in the people and the Constitution, and not the money. They're out there, just find them, and get what YOU PAID FOR, a representative government.

When I ran for president, I was told by a big businessman, "why would I donate to you, when I can buy and sell the party candidates on either side and get what I need," doesn't that tell you something? It told me something, money controls the people in Washington D.C., (that golden calf, of money and power) are what drive these people to vote on issues the way they do, not to represent the people back home who voted them in. Someone on a talk show said the same thing. A little bit different, but the same thing, money controls the way a bill written and why it is passed and what's in it, not if it has a benefit for Americans, but what the money people need in it to benefit themselves. We all know it, but yet we elect the same people in. We just ain't too bright, are we? One question no one asks is how much money have they stole from us. Social Security for one, it's suppose be in a locked box. Why do the always go there for money they need, not worrying about the fact that it's our money for retirement, that government suppose too protect, not send.

President Obama blames the people for the bad things that he says Americans have done, but if he'd looked for the truth and not the lies, he'd be smart enough to see that that last statement is telling you why most bad things come about. Politicians like him, who are bought and paid for by people, special interest groups, foreign governments,(against the law) big business, or anyone who can put the money up to elect them. They are the ones who get things do for them! How can we CHANGE that? Read on. Hollywood and special interest groups wanted the Keystone pipeline stopped, 100,000,000 dollars was promised to democrats in the last election. The thing that had to do was to promise to pass green energy laws. Bribe? Key stone stopped, EPA issues new regulation, the only losers are the American people. This from a President that said, "we the people are the ones in control." (ten times in his last oath of office speech), lies or just pulling the wool over your eyes?

(BRIBE: something (as money or favors) given or promised to a person or people to influence conduct, Webster's Dictionary)

The next subjects are going to be short, but to the point, but you're going have to think, answer the questions and make up your mind as to what you're going to do. But before you answer you may have to take a look at earlier chapters and what other things our founding fathers warned us about. If it goes against what you believe, why vote these people back in. Start looking for someone that believes in the Constitution, what was written in the Constitution and has knowledge about business is, religious freedom, freedom of speech and the bill pf rights, education is about and why it is failing.

Let's start with education. Why are home schooled kids, charter and private schooled kids better prepared for college then public schooled kids. Less money, lower pay, and better results, shouldn't we be asking why? Why are minority kids being cheated out of a good education, which includes good manners, time in the class, and be held accountable for their action, unless you want them to fail? Which is what the educate system is doing to them now. Education is taking the drive out of our minorities, and blaming on the past, the results are they learn to hate, and blame it on everything but the truth. They are getting cheated out of a future by the Democrats, who wants to enslave them to the government. I was a teacher for twenty years, vocational education, both in high school and college. The biggest problems, students coming into my classroom without the basic skills of reading, writing, and being able to do the math and the questions I ask is, how can they make it to this grade level without these skills? Why are our education systems not meeting the needs of our students to be successful in public education? Answer. GOVERNMENT CONTROL! Common core is the biggest jokes ever put in our educational system, but why are we putting it in?

It's not meeting the needs of the students but to destroy our educational systems. I explained this in more detail in the chapter IT'S TIME FOR A REALTY CHECK, WHY IS EDUCATION FAILING IN THIS COUNTRY? Read it. Even to find out more we've got to sit down and talk, because the truth about education, it has become no more than a place to educate our kids on government control. Just remember what our founding fathers said about education and freedom. Then you'll understand why education is failing to educate our children.

Health Care: Your better off losing one quarter of your wages and having your government help you pay for your health care, and not having a way to improve your life style. Great future, right! Cost going up and care and not down like promised, losing your doctors, and hospital as promised, big cost up front. Getting kicked off your company's health care program and now you'll have to pay for it. Getting fined at tax season for not having health care, add cost! (Going up every year from here on out.) Just a few of the great benefits promised by the President, Democrats, and now the Republican leadership. BUT THE BIGGEST BENEFIT IS NOW BEING TOLD YOU TO BUY IT FOR LIFE, GOOD OR BAD, YOU NO LONGER HAVE FREEDOM OF CHOICE, YOU'RE NOT SMART ENOUGH TO KNOW WHAT'S BETTER FOR YOU! JUST ASK THE GOVERNMENT, PRESIDENT OF THIS COUNTRY AND THE DEMOCRATS AND NOW THE REPUBLICANS. YOUR NOT SMART, JUST REMEMBER THAT, WE AIN'T TOO BRIGHT, ARE WE? (Why should a male have to buy birth control pill? It's in the law!) What wrong with this picture? Simple question, just ask yourself and you'll know the truth. Destroying our freedoms, because we just ain't too bright, are we? Another question should be how much COERCION, EXTORTION, and FRAUD was used to get it passed. There are three more words you can look up for their meaning.

How do you change health care for the better, simple? To change health care you can't start in Washington D.C., democrats or republicans have no clue as to what would work. Their answers come from, how to protect themselves from losing donations for re-election, not on how to make it better for Americans. They are not interested in we the people, but in those golden calves of money and power. If you really want to solve this problem, here's how you do it.

The people who don't have insurance, is not because of this country, but because of their choices in life and who they voted for. Their life style, their income, and many others reason, but not because of the country, the mismanagement of this country is the reason you're losing freedom of choice. All people in this country can receive medical attention, legal or illegal. This would give us our freedom of choice back. By doing this we established a system that again save cost, once again going to the free market, competition for services, equal lower rates. Not the joke we now have for medical care. It's driving the cost up every year from here on out, care going down, doctors leaving the profession because it's not about care but control over the people. Take a look at what we just said, answer your own questions. You'll find out who's screwing the American people. The elected people in Washington are the ones hurting the middle-class, not the country.

The last subject I'm going to cover is hate and prejudice, again, how can we end it in this country before it tears us apart and who wants hate and prejudice in this country for political reason only, because if ends they lose. Try people like Chris Mathews and how other new reporters blame everything on hate and prejudice. Earlier in this book I wrote about what to do to end it, and asked the question as to what do the black people own the white who died to set them free. They set them free to follow their dreams like any other American and that they are equal to every man. NOT TO BECOME ENSLAVED TO WELFARE, DRUGS, GANGS, POLITICAL PARTIES, WHO REALLY CARE NOTICE THING ABOUT THEM, BUT ONLY WANT THEIR VOTE. THE MOST IMPORTANT THING THEY MUST ANSWER IS WHO IS TELLING THEM THAT THEY ARE NOT EQUAL THAT THE GOVERNMENT WILL TAKE CARE OF THEM FOR THEIR VOTE. WHAT PARTY KEEPS TELL THEM THAT? ANSWER, THE DEMOCARTIC PARTY! SO WHO'S KEEP BLACK AMERICANS DOWN? It's not only the Democratic party, but the news media, the government and people who can profit from it. (You know who they are and the golden calf of money and power)

Fear and ignorance are the things that helps push it forward. But to make it clear I'm going to quote the President, in his own words, to explain it, "We are all created in God's image." THE IGNORANCE IS NOT BELEIVING IN THAT, AND LACK OF KNOWLEDGE OR UNDERSTANDING THAT. I guess the President doesn't understand his own words. There is only one race, THE HUMAN RACE, all men are equal unless you want to put them down. Don't ask the President that because he doesn't believe that. In his eyes, they are black, brown, yellow, red, white or any other color he wants. In GOD'S eyes there is only one race, again it's the human race.

Anytime they call a person black, African American, Hispanic, or anything else, they are looking down on you and telling you that you are not as good as them. Again who does that? News-media, Democrats, the President of the country and anyone who wants to put people down. To end it is simple: Americans are Americans, it doesn't matter what color you are. Eliminate the questions on race on all paper work. But if they eliminate it the Democratic party loses, the news-media lose, and the people who use it for profit lose but it ends. IT CAN NO LONGER BE USED IT TO DIVIDE AND CONQUER, THE AMERICAN CITIZEN FOR THEIR VOTES, FACTS WOULD GET THE VOTE, RESULTS WOULD GET THE VOTE, NOT THE LIES.

The answer to how do we change what's happening in our government is simple. Vote the parties out. Find candidates who believe in AMERICA and AMERICANS not parties. They are out their but they don't want to have to go out and ask people for money. If they had a resource to run set up by the people who believe them and their ideas. It would probably solve the problem, and save our country which is not a bad idea if that's what we want. Think about it, 10.00 dollars and your vote for congressman, 20.00 dollars for senators and your vote, and for president 100.00 dollars and your vote, so for 130.00 dollars you have bought the candidates that can change government for the better. Guest who this people will represent? WE THE PEOPLE, not we the party or the money but We THE PEOPLE, isn't that what you want. It would change Washington D.C. for the better.

Think about it and start looking for those candidates for true change. WE THE PEOPLE have got to be willing to put up the money.

Movies to watch: Pearl Harbor
       We were Soldiers
       They Dead with their Boots On

This book was written for three reasons. To let out my feelings of what's happening in this country, because I don't agree. To awake Americans to what is happening to their way of life and future because we ain't too bright. My doctor told me to do it to help my blood pressure. Yes I am angry, disgusted, and can't believe that Americans have done this to themselves. I hope if someone reads this book and it covers just how they feel and answers some of their questions to help them understand why the name "We ain't too bright, are we?"

The true reason I wrote it is because I am an American, believe in God, and believe in the Constitution and Bill of Rights and the freedom given to us by our forefathers. I read history and see what's happening here has happened before and not for the best interest of their country. When you don't learn from history you fail, as proven may times.

I want my sons and their families to enjoy the freedom I have enjoyed with them and I want them to enjoy the same things with their families. But most of all I want the future Americans to enjoy it too. The greatness of this country has been its people and not the government. It was founded as a government for the people and by the people. Not for the rich, special interest, or elite as some people believe they are. We are the government, not the elite, or rich, but people.

When you continue to use hate and prejudice to divide this country to gain power, remember this is not what this country was founded on, was it? When you continue to lie, distort the truth to gain money for your personal needs, off the backs of hard working Americans: when you no longer represent the people who elected you and put their trust in you, it time for a change. When you put Americans in debt, the future in debt without even reading the bill, it's not about Americans it's about you, the politicians, the greedy, the person with no standards just self-interest then we ain't too bright are we? Common sense has not been used for many years because they have trained us to think this way.

Americans, this is your country and you are the government. Remember that when you're paying taxes on special interest bill because of lies and in the name of your best interest, even if it's a lie. Remember, why you voted for a party that put you out of work, cause you to lose your home and made their supporters rich with their pay to play games. Now think I'm talking about both parties, not just one. Why would a 79 year old man want to run for office again and why would someone vote him in. We're just ain't too bright, are we? Make your own change; vote them all out.

When you deal from strength you're strong. When you give of yourself you make others better. When you deceive what a tangled web you weave. We are at a turning point in this country's history, will we fail and go down from here or will we fight back and rebuild our greatest for the future? The way to do that is to do the research, find someone that believes in Americans and not politicians. So if you really want to find out who they represent follow the money where it comes from and where it goes then you'll also find out the truth about your leadership. Then use your God given right and *vote* them out. Or you can go quietly into the night because you just not too bright and voted them back in. If you don't have the courage to do that, you'll never get change.

www.ingramcontent.com/pod-product-compliance
Lightning Source LLC
Chambersburg PA
CBHW021236280526
45784CB00005B/2115